# THIS JOURNAL BELONGS TO:

LoveofLink Publishers

# SOCIAL ACCOUNTS

## ACCOUNT MANAGEMENT

### FACEBOOK

**1**

URL

USERNAME:

PASSWORD:

### INSTAGRAM

**2**

URL:

USERNAME:

PASSWORD:

### PINTEREST

**3**

URL:

USERNAME:

PASSWORD:

### YOUTUBE

**4**

URL:

USERNAME:

PASSWORD:

### BLOG

**5**

URL:

USERNAME:

PASSWORD:

### LINKEDIN

**6**

URL:

USERNAME:

PASSWORD:

**7**

URL:

USERNAME:

PASSWORD:

**8**

URL:

USERNAME:

PASSWORD:

**9**

URL:

USERNAME:

PASSWORD:

**10**

URL:

USERNAME:

PASSWORD:

# BUSINESS GOALS

## QUARTERLY GOAL BREAKDOWN

QUARTER:  △ **1**  △ **2**  △ **3**  △ **4**     MONTH BEGINNING:

GOAL:

| ACTION STEPS |
| --- |
| |

MONTH:

| ACTION POINTS FOR COMPLETION |
| --- |
| |

MONTH:

| ACTION POINTS FOR COMPLETION |
| --- |
| |

MONTH:

# BUSINESS GOALS

## QUARTERLY GOALS & ACTION PLAN

QUARTER 1

QUARTER 2

QUARTER 3

QUARTER 4

## TOP GOALS PER CHANNEL/PLATFORM

- [ ] INSTAGRAM
- [ ] TWITTER
- [ ] PINTEREST
- [ ] FACEBOOK
- [ ] YOUTUBE
- [ ] TWITCH
- [ ] SNAPCHAT
- [ ] TUMBLR
- [ ] LINKEDIN
- [ ] BLOG
- [ ]

## NOTES & IDEAS

# TARGET AUDIENCE

## TARGET AUDIENCE SNAPSHOT AND MARKET OVERVIEW

**TARGET AUDIENCE OVERVIEW**

AGE

GENDER

LOCATION

EXPERIENCE LEVEL

OCCUPATION

EDUCATION

AVG MONTHLY INCOME

**NOTES**

**COMMONLY USED PLATFORMS**  ☐ ☐f ☐ ☐ ☐ ☐ ☐t ☐in ☐

OTHER INFORMATION:

### TOP PRODUCTS SOLD

- 
- 
- 
- 
- 

### TOP FACEBOOK GROUPS/FORUMS

- 
- 
- 
- 
- 

### TOP MARKET INFLUENCERS

- 
- 
- 
- 
- 

### TOP AUTHORITY BLOGGERS

- 
- 
- 
- 
- 

### NICHE RESEARCH NOTES

# BUSINESS CONTACTS

NAME

COMPANY

PHONE

EMAIL

NAME

COMPANY

PHONE

EMAIL

NAME

COMPANY

PHONE

EMAIL

NAME

COMPANY

PHONE

EMAIL

NAME

COMPANY

PHONE

EMAIL

NAME

COMPANY

PHONE

EMAIL

NAME

COMPANY

PHONE

EMAIL

NAME

COMPANY

PHONE

EMAIL

# WEEKLY PLANNER

## MONDAY

☐ BLOG ☐ TWITTER ☐ INSTAGRAM ☐ PINTEREST ☐ FACEBOOK

## TUESDAY

☐ BLOG ☐ TWITTER ☐ INSTAGRAM ☐ PINTEREST ☐ FACEBOOK

## WEDNESDAY

☐ BLOG ☐ TWITTER ☐ INSTAGRAM ☐ PINTEREST ☐ FACEBOOK

## THURSDAY

☐ BLOG ☐ TWITTER ☐ INSTAGRAM ☐ PINTEREST ☐ FACEBOOK

## FRIDAY

☐ BLOG ☐ TWITTER ☐ INSTAGRAM ☐ PINTEREST ☐ FACEBOOK

## SATURDAY

☐ BLOG ☐ TWITTER ☐ INSTAGRAM ☐ PINTEREST ☐ FACEBOOK

## SUNDAY

☐ BLOG ☐ TWITTER ☐ INSTAGRAM ☐ PINTEREST ☐ FACEBOOK

# WEEKLY PLANNER

**DATE:**

IDEAS, TOPICS, SUMMARY

| BLOG UPDATES/TOPICS | M | T | W | T | F | S | S | IDEAS FOR FUTURE UPDATES |
|---|---|---|---|---|---|---|---|---|
| | | | | | | | | |

# SOCAL MEDIA

## SOCIAL MEDIA SCHEDULE

|  | MONDAY | TUESDAY | WEDNESDAY | THURSDAY |
| --- | --- | --- | --- | --- |
| **FACEBOOK PAGE** | POSTED ☐ | POSTED ☐ | POSTED ☐ | POSTED ☐ |
| **YOUTUBE** | POSTED ☐ | POSTED ☐ | POSTED ☐ | POSTED ☐ |
| **INSTAGRAM** | POSTED ☐ | POSTED ☐ | POSTED ☐ | POSTED ☐ |
| **PINTEREST** | POSTED ☐ | POSTED ☐ | POSTED ☐ | POSTED ☐ |
| **TWITTER** | POSTED ☐ | POSTED ☐ | POSTED ☐ | POSTED ☐ |
| **BLOG** | POSTED ☐ | POSTED ☐ | POSTED ☐ | POSTED ☐ |

# SOCAL MEDIA

## SOCIAL MEDIA SCHEDULE

| | FRIDAY | SATURDAY | SUNDAY | NOTES |
|---|---|---|---|---|
| FACEBOOK PAGE | POSTED ☐ | POSTED ☐ | POSTED ☐ | |
| YOUTUBE | POSTED ☐ | POSTED ☐ | POSTED ☐ | |
| INSTAGRAM | POSTED ☐ | POSTED ☐ | POSTED ☐ | |
| PINTEREST | POSTED ☐ | POSTED ☐ | POSTED ☐ | |
| TWITTER | POSTED ☐ | POSTED ☐ | POSTED ☐ | |
| BLOG | POSTED ☐ | POSTED ☐ | POSTED ☐ | |

# SOCIAL TASKS

## SOCIAL MEDIA TASK TRACKER

| ACTION/TASK | MON | TUE | WED | THU | FRI | SAT | SUN |
|---|---|---|---|---|---|---|---|
| | | | | | | | |
| | | | | | | | |
| | | | | | | | |
| | | | | | | | |
| | | | | | | | |
| | | | | | | | |
| | | | | | | | |
| | | | | | | | |
| | | | | | | | |
| | | | | | | | |

# CONTENT PLANNER

## BLOG & SOCIAL MEDIA CONTENT PLANNER

| DETAILS | DATE | PLATFORM | DONE |
|---|---|---|---|
| | | | |

# ADVERTISING



PAID ADVERTISING – PLANNER & TRACKER

---

AD SUBJECT: | PUBLISHED: | DURATION:

CONTENT:

☐ TWITTER ☐ INSTAGRAM ☐ PINTEREST ☐ FACEBOOK ☐ OTHER

BUDGET: | CLICKS: | REACH: | VIEWS: | CTR:

---

AD SUBJECT: | PUBLISHED: | DURATION:

CONTENT:

☐ TWITTER ☐ INSTAGRAM ☐ PINTEREST ☐ FACEBOOK ☐ OTHER

BUDGET: | CLICKS: | REACH: | VIEWS: | CTR:

---

AD SUBJECT: | PUBLISHED: | DURATION:

CONTENT:

☐ TWITTER ☐ INSTAGRAM ☐ PINTEREST ☐ FACEBOOK ☐ OTHER

BUDGET: | CLICKS: | REACH: | VIEWS: | CTR:

---

AD SUBJECT: | PUBLISHED: | DURATION:

CONTENT:

☐ TWITTER ☐ INSTAGRAM ☐ PINTEREST ☐ FACEBOOK ☐ OTHER

BUDGET: | CLICKS: | REACH: | VIEWS: | CTR:

# SOCIAL MEDIA

## SOCIAL MEDIA ACCOUNT MANAGEMENT

| SOCIAL MEDIA ACCOUNTS | FACEBOOK GROUPS/OUTREACH |
|---|---|
| FACEBOOK.COM/ | |
| TWITTER: @ | |
| PINTEREST.COM/ | |
| INSTAGRAM.COM/ | |
| YOUTUBE.COM/ | |

## SOCIAL MEDIA NOTES & IDEAS GOING FORWARD

## OTHER SOCIAL MEDIA ACCOUNTS

| CHANNEL | URL | USERNAME | PASSWORD |
|---|---|---|---|
| | | | |
| | | | |
| | | | |
| | | | |

# SPONSORSHIPS

## PAID SPONSORSHIPS AND REVIEWS

COMPANY / BUSINESS:

PRODUCT

CONTACT

OVERVIEW

KEYWORDS & LINKS

PUBLISH DATE      /      /                    INCOME

NOTES                                         THOUGHTS/OVERVIEW

---

COMPANY / BUSINESS:

PRODUCT

CONTACT

OVERVIEW

KEYWORDS & LINKS

PUBLISH DATE      /      /                    INCOME

NOTES                                         THOUGHTS/OVERVIEW

---

COMPANY / BUSINESS:

PRODUCT

CONTACT

OVERVIEW

KEYWORDS & LINKS

PUBLISH DATE      /      /                    INCOME

NOTES                                         THOUGHTS/OVERVIEW

# CONTENT PLANNER

## SOCIAL MEDIA CONTENT PLANNER

### MONDAY

### TUESDAY

### WEDNESDAY

### THURSDAY

### FRIDAY

### SATURDAY

### SUNDAY

### NOTES & REMINDERS

# POST PLANNER

BLOG POST PLANNER

POST TITLE:

POSTING DATE:

TYPE/FORMAT: ARTICLE ☐ REVIEW ☐ TUTORIAL ☐ SPONSORED ☐ GUEST POST ☐

BLOG POST OVERVIEW/SUMMARY

| BLOG POST IDEAS FOR THE MONTH | NEWSLETTER/MAILING LIST PROMO |
| --- | --- |

| OTHER PROMOTIONAL CHANNELS |
| --- |

| MONTHLY REFLECTION | IDEAS TO GROW TRAFFIC NEXT MONTH |
| --- | --- |

| ADVERTISING & PROMOTION | TAGS & KEYWORDS |
| --- | --- |

| RESEARCH | SOURCES |
| --- | --- |

| CROSS POSTING & GUEST BLOGGING | SOCIAL MEDIA |
| --- | --- |

FUTURE FOLLOW UP / CROSS MARKETING IDEAS

# NEWSLETTER OUTREACH

## NEWSLETTER TRACKER

NEWSLETTER TOPIC:                                    PUBLISHED:

CONTENT:

# SUBSCRIBERS:              OPEN RATES:              CTR:

NEWSLETTER TOPIC:                                    PUBLISHED:

CONTENT:

# SUBSCRIBERS:              OPEN RATES:              CTR:

NEWSLETTER TOPIC:                                    PUBLISHED:

CONTENT:

# SUBSCRIBERS:              OPEN RATES:              CTR:

NEWSLETTER TOPIC:                                    PUBLISHED:

CONTENT:

# SUBSCRIBERS:              OPEN RATES:              CTR:

### FUTURE NEWSLETTER SUBJECT LINES & IDEAS

# MARKETING

## ADVERTISING IDEAS TO MAXIMIZE OUTREACH

| SOCIAL MEDIA FOCUS: | MARKETING CHANNELS | ADVERTISING FOCUS |
|---|---|---|
| ☐ INSTAGRAM | | |
| ☐ TWITTER | | |
| ☐ PINTEREST | | |
| ☐ FACEBOOK | | |
| ☐ YOUTUBE | | |
| ☐ TWITCH | | |
| ☐ SNAPCHAT | | |
| ☐ LINKEDIN | | |
| ☐ BLOG | | |
| ☐ | | |
| ☐ | | |

## MARKETING STRATEGY

**CHANNEL**

**TARGET GOAL**

**MARKETING IDEAS**

**ACTION PLAN**

# LINKED IN POSTS

## LINKEDIN POSTS & UPDATE PLANNER

**POST**

| SUMMARY | | PUBLISHED  /  / |
|---|---|---|
| | | SPONSORED / PAID BY |
| | | REMINDERS & TO DO |
| | | ☐ |
| | | ☐ |
| TAGS | HASHTAGS | ☐ |
| @ | # | ☐ |
| @ | # | ☐ |
| @ | # | ☐ |

**POST**

| SUMMARY | | PUBLISHED  /  / |
|---|---|---|
| | | SPONSORED BY |
| | | REMINDERS & TO DO |
| | | ☐ |
| | | ☐ |
| TAGS | HASHTAGS | ☐ |
| @ | # | ☐ |
| @ | # | ☐ |
| @ | # | ☐ |

**POST**

| SUMMARY | | PUBLISHED  /  / |
|---|---|---|
| | | SPONSORED BY |
| | | REMINDERS & TO DO |
| | | ☐ |
| | | ☐ |
| TAGS | HASHTAGS | ☐ |
| @ | # | ☐ |
| @ | # | ☐ |
| @ | # | ☐ |

# INSTAGRAM POSTS

## INSTAGRAM POSTS & UPDATE PLANNER

**POST TITLE:**

SUMMARY:

PUBLISHED ON: / /

SPONSORED/PAID BY:

REMINDERS & TO DO

TAGS

LINKS     HASHTAGS

@     #

@     #

@     #

**POST TITLE:**

SUMMARY:

PUBLISHED ON: / /

SPONSORED/PAID BY:

REMINDERS & TO DO

TAGS

LINKS     HASHTAGS

@     #

@     #

@     #

**POST TITLE:**

SUMMARY:

PUBLISHED ON: / /

SPONSORED/PAID BY:

REMINDERS & TO DO

TAGS

LINKS     HASHTAGS

@     #

@     #

@     #

# PINTEREST PLANNER

## PINTEREST VISION BOARD AND PLANNER

| BOARD #1 | BOARD #2 | BOARD #3 | BOARD #4 | BOARD #5 |
|---|---|---|---|---|

| BOARD #6 | BOARD #7 | BOARD #8 | BOARD #9 | BOARD #10 |
|---|---|---|---|---|

### Top Performing Pins

### What's Currently Trending on Pinterest?

### Most Popular Boards

### Pins to Revive

### Main Keywords

### Included Elements

- [ ] BLOG POSTS
- [ ] SPONSORS
- [ ] ETSY
- [ ] TESTIMONIALS
- [ ] REVIEW
- [ ] SPOTLIGHT

### Notes

# PINTEREST PLANNER

## PINTEREST MARKETING PLANNER

**FOLLOWING**

**DAILY PIN GOAL**

### TOP PINS OF THE WEEK

### TOP KEYWORDS OF THE WEEK

| MONDAY | TUESDAY | WEDNESDAY | THURSDAY |
|--------|---------|-----------|----------|
| KEYWORDS | KEYWORDS | KEYWORDS | KEYWORDS |

| FRIDAY | SATURDAY | SUNDAY | NOTES |
|--------|----------|--------|-------|
| KEYWORDS | KEYWORDS | KEYWORDS | KEYWORDS |

# FACEBOOK PLANNER

## FACEBOOK MARKETING PLANNER

**FOLLOWING**

**TARGET GOAL**

### SCHEDULED POSTS

### TOP POSTS

**MONDAY**

**TUESDAY**

**WEDNESDAY**

**THURSDAY**

TRAFFIC STATS

TRAFFIC STATS

TRAFFIC STATS

TRAFFIC STATS

**FRIDAY**

**SATURDAY**

**SUNDAY**

**NOTES**

TRAFFIC STATS

TRAFFIC STATS

TRAFFIC STATS

TRAFFIC STATS

# YOUTUBE UPDATES

SUMMARY OF UPDATE

☐ FILMED ☐ EDITED ☐ THUMBNAIL ☐ DESCRIPTION ☐ PUBLISHED

SUMMARY OF UPDATE

☐ FILMED ☐ EDITED ☐ THUMBNAIL ☐ DESCRIPTION ☐ PUBLISHED

SUMMARY OF UPDATE

☐ FILMED ☐ EDITED ☐ THUMBNAIL ☐ DESCRIPTION ☐ PUBLISHED

SUMMARY OF UPDATE

☐ FILMED ☐ EDITED ☐ THUMBNAIL ☐ DESCRIPTION ☐ PUBLISHED

SUMMARY OF UPDATE

☐ FILMED ☐ EDITED ☐ THUMBNAIL ☐ DESCRIPTION ☐ PUBLISHED

SUMMARY OF UPDATE

☐ FILMED ☐ EDITED ☐ THUMBNAIL ☐ DESCRIPTION ☐ PUBLISHED

SUMMARY OF UPDATE

☐ FILMED ☐ EDITED ☐ THUMBNAIL ☐ DESCRIPTION ☐ PUBLISHED

# SPONSORED POSTS

## PAID SPONSORSHIPS & POSTS

| COMPANY | REVIEW | DEADLINE | EARNINGS | COMPLETED |
| --- | --- | --- | --- | --- |
|  |  |  |  |  |
|  |  |  |  |  |
|  |  |  |  |  |
|  |  |  |  |  |
|  |  |  |  |  |
|  |  |  |  |  |
|  |  |  |  |  |
|  |  |  |  |  |
|  |  |  |  |  |
|  |  |  |  |  |

# HASHTAG IDEAS

## HASHTAGS RESEARCH AND IDEAS

**POST THEME:**

Tag #1

Tag #2

Tag #3

Tag #4

Tag #5

Tag #6

Tag #7

Tag #8

**POST THEME:**

Tag #1

Tag #2

Tag #3

Tag #4

Tag #5

Tag #6

Tag #7

Tag #8

**POST THEME:**

Tag #1

Tag #2

Tag #3

Tag #4

Tag #5

Tag #6

Tag #7

Tag #8

**POST THEME:**

Tag #1

Tag #2

Tag #3

Tag #4

Tag #5

Tag #6

Tag #7

Tag #8

**POST THEME:**

Tag #1

Tag #2

Tag #3

Tag #4

Tag #5

Tag #6

Tag #7

Tag #8

**POST THEME:**

Tag #1

Tag #2

Tag #3

Tag #4

Tag #5

Tag #6

Tag #7

Tag #8

# SOCIAL MEDIA

## SOCIAL MEDIA UPDATE TRACKER

**DATE**　　　　　☐ CONTENT　　☐ PHOTO / VIDEO

OTHER

**DATE**　　　　　☐ CONTENT　　☐ PHOTO / VIDEO

OTHER

**DATE**　　　　　☐ CONTENT　　☐ PHOTO / VIDEO

OTHER

**DATE**　　　　　☐ CONTENT　　☐ PHOTO / VIDEO

OTHER

**DATE**　　　　　☐ CONTENT　　☐ PHOTO / VIDEO

OTHER

# DATA ANALYSIS

## BUSINESS GROWTH, DATA CHARTS, PROGRESS

CHART FOR:

CHART FOR:

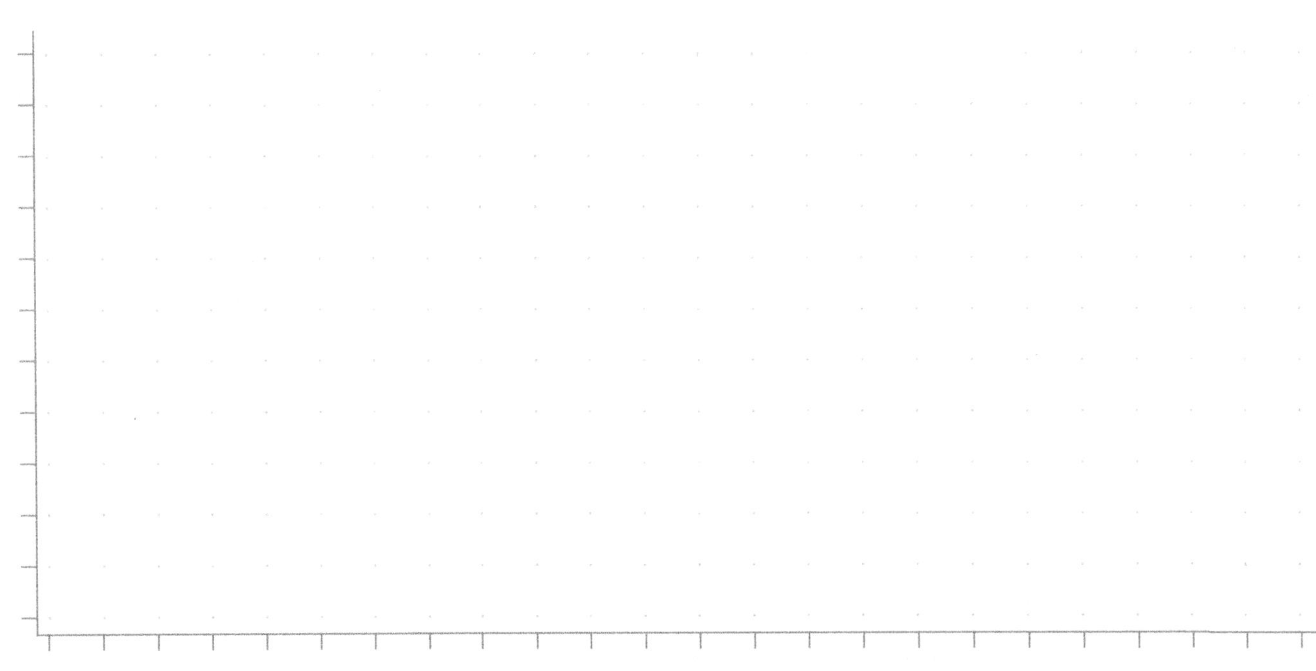

# WEEKLY PLANNER

## MONDAY

BLOG  TWITTER  INSTAGRAM  PINTEREST  FACEBOOK

## TUESDAY

BLOG  TWITTER  INSTAGRAM  PINTEREST  FACEBOOK

## WEDNESDAY

BLOG  TWITTER  INSTAGRAM  PINTEREST  FACEBOOK

## THURSDAY

BLOG  TWITTER  INSTAGRAM  PINTEREST  FACEBOOK

## FRIDAY

BLOG  TWITTER  INSTAGRAM  PINTEREST  FACEBOOK

## SATURDAY

BLOG  TWITTER  INSTAGRAM  PINTEREST  FACEBOOK

## SUNDAY

BLOG  TWITTER  INSTAGRAM  PINTEREST  FACEBOOK

# WEEKLY PLANNER

**DATE:**

IDEAS, TOPICS, SUMMARY

BLOG UPDATES/TOPICS

M T W T F S S

IDEAS FOR FUTURE UPDATES

# SOCAL MEDIA

## SOCIAL MEDIA SCHEDULE

| | MONDAY | TUESDAY | WEDNESDAY | THURSDAY |
|---|---|---|---|---|
| **FACEBOOK PAGE** | POSTED ☐ | POSTED ☐ | POSTED ☐ | POSTED ☐ |
| **YOUTUBE** | POSTED ☐ | POSTED ☐ | POSTED ☐ | POSTED ☐ |
| **INSTAGRAM** | POSTED ☐ | POSTED ☐ | POSTED ☐ | POSTED ☐ |
| **PINTEREST** | POSTED ☐ | POSTED ☐ | POSTED ☐ | POSTED ☐ |
| **TWITTER** | POSTED ☐ | POSTED ☐ | POSTED ☐ | POSTED ☐ |
| **BLOG** | POSTED ☐ | POSTED ☐ | POSTED ☐ | POSTED ☐ |

# SOCAL MEDIA

## SOCIAL MEDIA SCHEDULE

|  | FRIDAY | SATURDAY | SUNDAY | NOTES |
|---|---|---|---|---|
| **FACEBOOK PAGE** | POSTED ☐ | POSTED ☐ | POSTED ☐ | |
| **YOUTUBE** | POSTED ☐ | POSTED ☐ | POSTED ☐ | |
| **INSTAGRAM** | POSTED ☐ | POSTED ☐ | POSTED ☐ | |
| **PINTEREST** | POSTED ☐ | POSTED ☐ | POSTED ☐ | |
| **TWITTER** | POSTED ☐ | POSTED ☐ | POSTED ☐ | |
| **BLOG** | POSTED ☐ | POSTED ☐ | POSTED ☐ | |

# SOCIAL TASKS

## SOCIAL MEDIA TASK TRACKER

| ACTION/TASK | MON | TUE | WED | THU | FRI | SAT | SUN |
|---|---|---|---|---|---|---|---|
| | | | | | | | |

# CONTENT PLANNER

## BLOG & SOCIAL MEDIA CONTENT PLANNER

| DETAILS | DATE | PLATFORM | DONE |
|---|---|---|---|
|  |  |  |  |
|  |  |  |  |
|  |  |  |  |
|  |  |  |  |
|  |  |  |  |
|  |  |  |  |
|  |  |  |  |
|  |  |  |  |
|  |  |  |  |
|  |  |  |  |
|  |  |  |  |
|  |  |  |  |
|  |  |  |  |
|  |  |  |  |
|  |  |  |  |
|  |  |  |  |
|  |  |  |  |
|  |  |  |  |
|  |  |  |  |
|  |  |  |  |

# ADVERTISING

PAID ADVERTISING – PLANNER & TRACKER

AD SUBJECT:     PUBLISHED:     DURATION:

CONTENT:

☐ TWITTER     ☐ INSTAGRAM     ☐ PINTEREST     ☐ FACEBOOK     ☐ OTHER

BUDGET:     CLICKS:     REACH:     VIEWS:     CTR:

---

AD SUBJECT:     PUBLISHED:     DURATION:

CONTENT:

☐ TWITTER     ☐ INSTAGRAM     ☐ PINTEREST     ☐ FACEBOOK     ☐ OTHER

BUDGET:     CLICKS:     REACH:     VIEWS:     CTR:

---

AD SUBJECT:     PUBLISHED:     DURATION:

CONTENT:

☐ TWITTER     ☐ INSTAGRAM     ☐ PINTEREST     ☐ FACEBOOK     ☐ OTHER

BUDGET:     CLICKS:     REACH:     VIEWS:     CTR:

---

AD SUBJECT:     PUBLISHED:     DURATION:

CONTENT:

☐ TWITTER     ☐ INSTAGRAM     ☐ PINTEREST     ☐ FACEBOOK     ☐ OTHER

BUDGET:     CLICKS:     REACH:     VIEWS:     CTR:

# SOCIAL MEDIA

## SOCIAL MEDIA ACCOUNT MANAGEMENT

| SOCIAL MEDIA ACCOUNTS | FACEBOOK GROUPS/OUTREACH |
|---|---|

FACEBOOK.COM/

TWITTER: @

PINTEREST.COM/

INSTAGRAM.COM/

YOUTUBE.COM/

## SOCIAL MEDIA NOTES & IDEAS GOING FORWARD

## OTHER SOCIAL MEDIA ACCOUNTS

| CHANNEL | URL | USERNAME | PASSWORD |
|---|---|---|---|
| | | | |
| | | | |
| | | | |
| | | | |
| | | | |

# SPONSORSHIPS

## PAID SPONSORSHIPS AND REVIEWS

COMPANY / BUSINESS:

PRODUCT

CONTACT

OVERVIEW

KEYWORDS & LINKS

PUBLISH DATE        /        /

NOTES

INCOME

THOUGHTS/OVERVIEW

---

COMPANY / BUSINESS:

PRODUCT

CONTACT

OVERVIEW

KEYWORDS & LINKS

PUBLISH DATE        /        /

NOTES

INCOME

THOUGHTS/OVERVIEW

---

COMPANY / BUSINESS:

PRODUCT

CONTACT

OVERVIEW

KEYWORDS & LINKS

PUBLISH DATE        /        /

NOTES

INCOME

THOUGHTS/OVERVIEW

# CONTENT PLANNER

## SOCIAL MEDIA CONTENT PLANNER

### MONDAY

### TUESDAY

### WEDNESDAY

### THURSDAY

### FRIDAY

### SATURDAY

### SUNDAY

### NOTES & REMINDERS

# POST PLANNER

BLOG POST PLANNER

POST TITLE:                                      POSTING DATE:

TYPE/FORMAT:   ARTICLE ☐      REVIEW ☐      TUTORIAL ☐      SPONSORED ☐      GUEST POST ☐

BLOG POST OVERVIEW/SUMMARY

| BLOG POST IDEAS FOR THE MONTH | NEWSLETTER/MAILING LIST PROMO |
| --- | --- |

| MONTHLY REFLECTION | IDEAS TO GROW TRAFFIC NEXT MONTH |
| --- | --- |

**OTHER PROMOTIONAL CHANNELS**

<table>
<tr><td>ADVERTISING & PROMOTION</td><td>TAGS & KEYWORDS</td></tr>
<tr><td>RESEARCH</td><td>SOURCES</td></tr>
<tr><td>CROSS POSTING & GUEST BLOGGING</td><td>SOCIAL MEDIA</td></tr>
</table>

FUTURE FOLLOW UP / CROSS MARKETING IDEAS

# NEWSLETTER OUTREACH

## NEWSLETTER TRACKER

NEWSLETTER TOPIC: | PUBLISHED:

CONTENT:

# SUBSCRIBERS: | OPEN RATES: | CTR:

NEWSLETTER TOPIC: | PUBLISHED:

CONTENT:

# SUBSCRIBERS: | OPEN RATES: | CTR:

NEWSLETTER TOPIC: | PUBLISHED:

CONTENT:

# SUBSCRIBERS: | OPEN RATES: | CTR:

NEWSLETTER TOPIC: | PUBLISHED:

CONTENT:

# SUBSCRIBERS: | OPEN RATES: | CTR:

### FUTURE NEWSLETTER SUBJECT LINES & IDEAS

# MARKING... 

# MARKETING

## ADVERTISING IDEAS TO MAXIMIZE OUTREACH

| SOCIAL MEDIA FOCUS: | MARKETING CHANNELS | ADVERTISING FOCUS |
|---|---|---|
| ☐ INSTAGRAM | | |
| ☐ TWITTER | | |
| ☐ PINTEREST | | |
| ☐ FACEBOOK | | |
| ☐ YOUTUBE | | |
| ☐ TWITCH | | |
| ☐ SNAPCHAT | | |
| ☐ LINKEDIN | | |
| ☐ BLOG | | |
| ☐ | | |
| ☐ | | |

## MARKETING STRATEGY

**CHANNEL**

**TARGET GOAL**

**MARKETING IDEAS**

**ACTION PLAN**

# LINKED IN POSTS

## LINKEDIN POSTS & UPDATE PLANNER

**POST**

| SUMMARY | PUBLISHED / / |
| --- | --- |
| | SPONSORED / PAID BY |
| | REMINDERS & TO DO |
| | ☐ |
| | ☐ |
| TAGS　　　HASHTAGS | ☐ |
| @　　　# | ☐ |
| @　　　# | ☐ |
| @　　　# | ☐ |

**POST**

| SUMMARY | PUBLISHED / / |
| --- | --- |
| | SPONSORED BY |
| | REMINDERS & TO DO |
| | ☐ |
| | ☐ |
| TAGS　　　HASHTAGS | ☐ |
| @　　　# | ☐ |
| @　　　# | ☐ |
| @　　　# | ☐ |

**POST**

| SUMMARY | PUBLISHED / / |
| --- | --- |
| | SPONSORED BY |
| | REMINDERS & TO DO |
| | ☐ |
| | ☐ |
| TAGS　　　HASHTAGS | ☐ |
| @　　　# | ☐ |
| @　　　# | ☐ |
| @　　　# | ☐ |

# INSTAGRAM POSTS

## INSTAGRAM POSTS & UPDATE PLANNER

**POST TITLE:**

| SUMMARY: | | PUBLISHED ON:  /  / |
| --- | --- | --- |
| | | SPONSORED/PAID BY: |
| | | REMINDERS & TO DO |
| | | ☐ |
| TAGS | | ☐ |
| LINKS | HASHTAGS | ☐ |
| @ | # | ☐ |
| @ | # | ☐ |
| @ | # | ☐ |

**POST TITLE:**

| SUMMARY: | | PUBLISHED ON:  /  / |
| --- | --- | --- |
| | | SPONSORED/PAID BY: |
| | | REMINDERS & TO DO |
| | | ☐ |
| TAGS | | ☐ |
| LINKS | HASHTAGS | ☐ |
| @ | # | ☐ |
| @ | # | ☐ |
| @ | # | ☐ |

**POST TITLE:**

| SUMMARY: | | PUBLISHED ON:  /  / |
| --- | --- | --- |
| | | SPONSORED/PAID BY: |
| | | REMINDERS & TO DO |
| | | ☐ |
| TAGS | | ☐ |
| LINKS | HASHTAGS | ☐ |
| @ | # | ☐ |
| @ | # | ☐ |
| @ | # | ☐ |

# PINTEREST PLANNER

## PINTEREST VISION BOARD AND PLANNER

| BOARD #1 | BOARD #2 | BOARD #3 | BOARD #4 | BOARD #5 |
|---|---|---|---|---|

| BOARD #6 | BOARD #7 | BOARD #8 | BOARD #9 | BOARD #10 |
|---|---|---|---|---|

### Top Performing Pins

### What's Currently Trending on Pinterest?

### Most Popular Boards

### Pins to Revive

### Main Keywords

### Included Elements

- [ ] BLOG POSTS
- [ ] SPONSORS
- [ ] ETSY
- [ ] TESTIMONIALS
- [ ] REVIEW
- [ ] SPOTLIGHT

### Notes

# PINTEREST PLANNER

## PINTEREST MARKETING PLANNER

**FOLLOWING**

**DAILY PIN GOAL**

### TOP PINS OF THE WEEK

### TOP KEYWORDS OF THE WEEK

**MONDAY**

**TUESDAY**

**WEDNESDAY**

**THURSDAY**

KEYWORDS

KEYWORDS

KEYWORDS

KEYWORDS

**FRIDAY**

**SATURDAY**

**SUNDAY**

**NOTES**

KEYWORDS

KEYWORDS

KEYWORDS

KEYWORDS

# FACEBOOK PLANNER

## FACEBOOK MARKETING PLANNER

**FOLLOWING**

**TARGET GOAL**

### SCHEDULED POSTS

### TOP POSTS

| MONDAY | TUESDAY | WEDNESDAY | THURSDAY |
|---|---|---|---|
| TRAFFIC STATS | TRAFFIC STATS | TRAFFIC STATS | TRAFFIC STATS |

| FRIDAY | SATURDAY | SUNDAY | NOTES |
|---|---|---|---|
| TRAFFIC STATS | TRAFFIC STATS | TRAFFIC STATS | TRAFFIC STATS |

# YOUTUBE UPDATES

SUMMARY OF UPDATE

FILMED  EDITED  THUMBNAIL  DESCRIPTION  PUBLISHED

SUMMARY OF UPDATE

FILMED  EDITED  THUMBNAIL  DESCRIPTION  PUBLISHED

SUMMARY OF UPDATE

FILMED  EDITED  THUMBNAIL  DESCRIPTION  PUBLISHED

SUMMARY OF UPDATE

FILMED  EDITED  THUMBNAIL  DESCRIPTION  PUBLISHED

SUMMARY OF UPDATE

FILMED  EDITED  THUMBNAIL  DESCRIPTION  PUBLISHED

SUMMARY OF UPDATE

FILMED  EDITED  THUMBNAIL  DESCRIPTION  PUBLISHED

SUMMARY OF UPDATE

FILMED  EDITED  THUMBNAIL  DESCRIPTION  PUBLISHED

# SPONSORED POSTS

## PAID SPONSORSHIPS & POSTS

| COMPANY | REVIEW | DEADLINE | EARNINGS | COMPLETED |
|---------|--------|----------|----------|-----------|
|  |  |  |  |  |
|  |  |  |  |  |
|  |  |  |  |  |
|  |  |  |  |  |
|  |  |  |  |  |
|  |  |  |  |  |
|  |  |  |  |  |
|  |  |  |  |  |
|  |  |  |  |  |
|  |  |  |  |  |
|  |  |  |  |  |
|  |  |  |  |  |
|  |  |  |  |  |
|  |  |  |  |  |
|  |  |  |  |  |
|  |  |  |  |  |
|  |  |  |  |  |
|  |  |  |  |  |

# HASHTAG IDEAS

## HASHTAGS RESEARCH AND IDEAS

**POST THEME:**

Tag #1

Tag #2

Tag #3

Tag #4

Tag #5

Tag #6

Tag #7

Tag #8

**POST THEME:**

Tag #1

Tag #2

Tag #3

Tag #4

Tag #5

Tag #6

Tag #7

Tag #8

**POST THEME:**

Tag #1

Tag #2

Tag #3

Tag #4

Tag #5

Tag #6

Tag #7

Tag #8

**POST THEME:**

Tag #1

Tag #2

Tag #3

Tag #4

Tag #5

Tag #6

Tag #7

Tag #8

**POST THEME:**

Tag #1

Tag #2

Tag #3

Tag #4

Tag #5

Tag #6

Tag #7

Tag #8

**POST THEME:**

Tag #1

Tag #2

Tag #3

Tag #4

Tag #5

Tag #6

Tag #7

Tag #8

## SOCIAL MEDIA UPDATE TRACKER

---

DATE     ☐ CONTENT     ☐ PHOTO / VIDEO

OTHER

---

DATE     ☐ CONTENT     ☐ PHOTO / VIDEO

OTHER

---

DATE     ☐ CONTENT     ☐ PHOTO / VIDEO

OTHER

---

DATE     ☐ CONTENT     ☐ PHOTO / VIDEO

OTHER

---

DATE     ☐ CONTENT     ☐ PHOTO / VIDEO

OTHER

# DATA ANALYSIS

## BUSINESS GROWTH, DATA CHARTS, PROGRESS

CHART FOR:

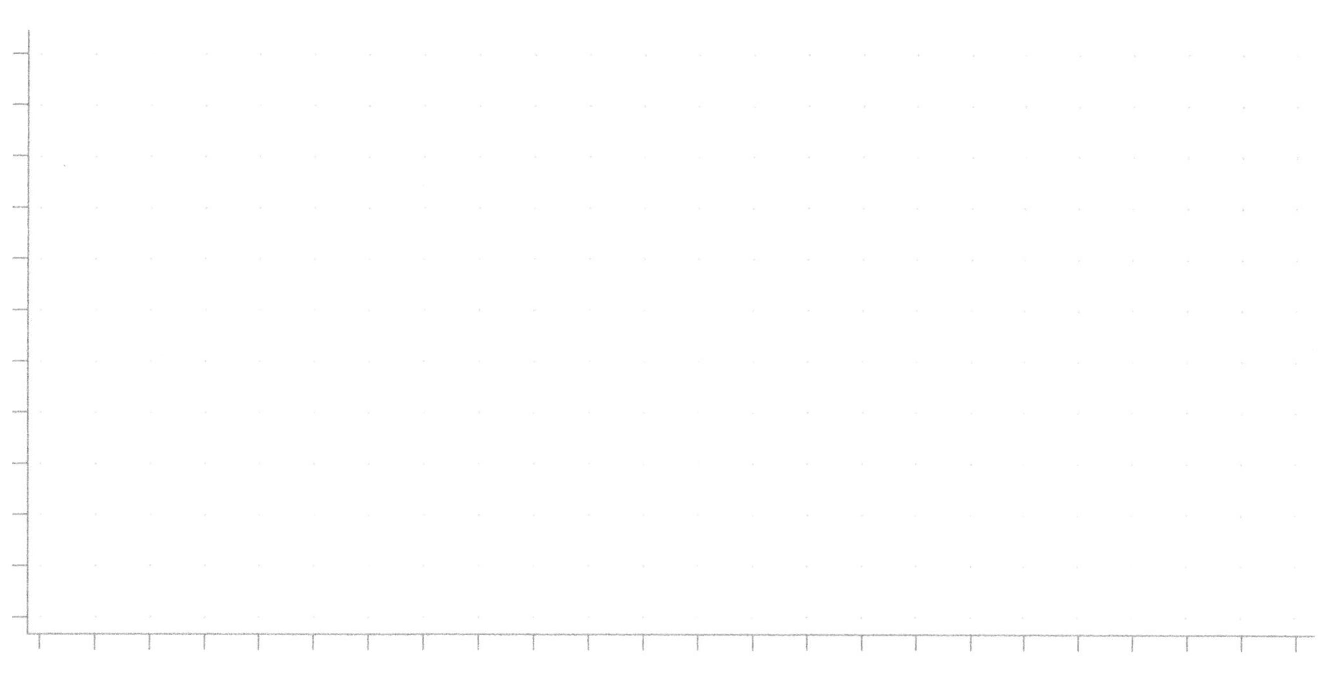

CHART FOR:

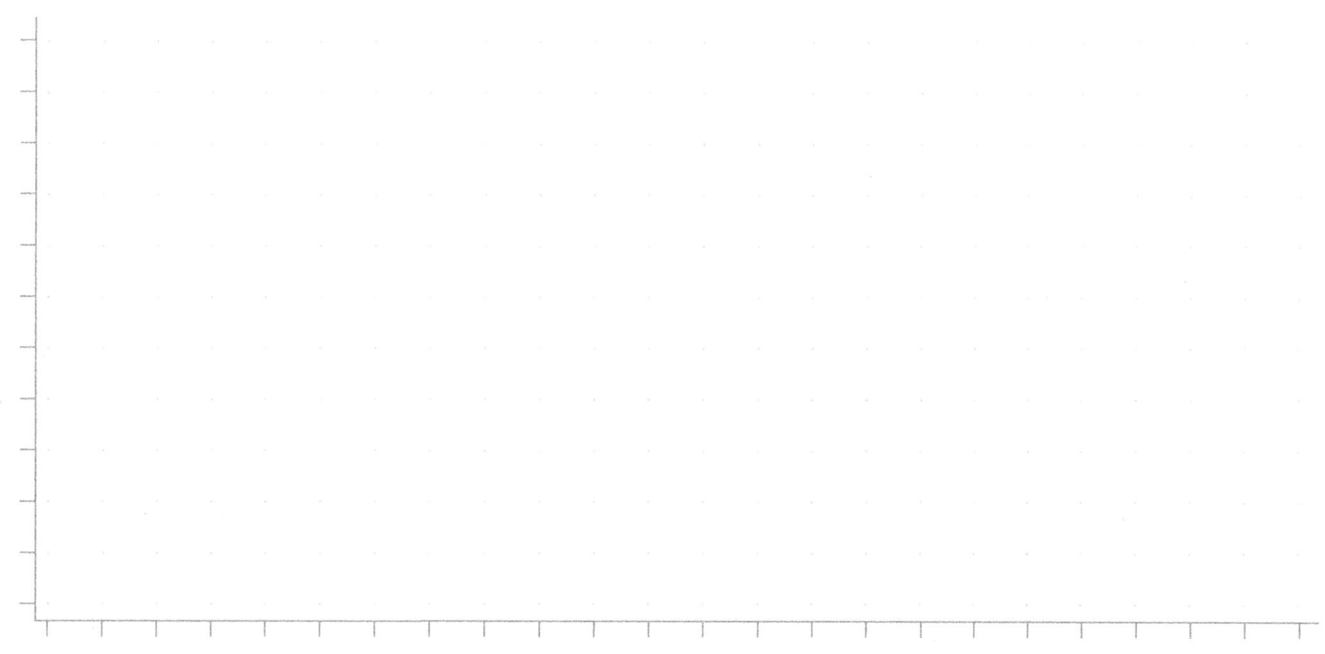

# WEEKLY PLANNER

## MONDAY

☐ BLOG ☐ TWITTER ☐ INSTAGRAM ☐ PINTEREST ☐ FACEBOOK

## TUESDAY

☐ BLOG ☐ TWITTER ☐ INSTAGRAM ☐ PINTEREST ☐ FACEBOOK

## WEDNESDAY

☐ BLOG ☐ TWITTER ☐ INSTAGRAM ☐ PINTEREST ☐ FACEBOOK

## THURSDAY

☐ BLOG ☐ TWITTER ☐ INSTAGRAM ☐ PINTEREST ☐ FACEBOOK

## FRIDAY

☐ BLOG ☐ TWITTER ☐ INSTAGRAM ☐ PINTEREST ☐ FACEBOOK

## SATURDAY

☐ BLOG ☐ TWITTER ☐ INSTAGRAM ☐ PINTEREST ☐ FACEBOOK

## SUNDAY

☐ BLOG ☐ TWITTER ☐ INSTAGRAM ☐ PINTEREST ☐ FACEBOOK

# WEEKLY PLANNER

**DATE:**

IDEAS, TOPICS, SUMMARY

| BLOG UPDATES/TOPICS | M | T | W | T | F | S | S | IDEAS FOR FUTURE UPDATES |
|---|---|---|---|---|---|---|---|---|
| | | | | | | | | |

# SOCAL MEDIA

## SOCIAL MEDIA SCHEDULE

| | MONDAY | TUESDAY | WEDNESDAY | THURSDAY |
|---|---|---|---|---|
| FACEBOOK PAGE | POSTED ☐ | POSTED ☐ | POSTED ☐ | POSTED ☐ |
| YOUTUBE | POSTED ☐ | POSTED ☐ | POSTED ☐ | POSTED ☐ |
| INSTAGRAM | POSTED ☐ | POSTED ☐ | POSTED ☐ | POSTED ☐ |
| PINTEREST | POSTED ☐ | POSTED ☐ | POSTED ☐ | POSTED ☐ |
| TWITTER | POSTED ☐ | POSTED ☐ | POSTED ☐ | POSTED ☐ |
| BLOG | POSTED ☐ | POSTED ☐ | POSTED ☐ | POSTED ☐ |

# SOCAL MEDIA

## SOCIAL MEDIA SCHEDULE

| | FRIDAY | SATURDAY | SUNDAY | NOTES |
|---|---|---|---|---|
| **FACEBOOK PAGE** | POSTED | POSTED | POSTED | |
| **YOUTUBE** | POSTED | POSTED | POSTED | |
| **INSTAGRAM** | POSTED | POSTED | POSTED | |
| **PINTEREST** | POSTED | POSTED | POSTED | |
| **TWITTER** | POSTED | POSTED | POSTED | |
| **BLOG** | POSTED | POSTED | POSTED | |

# SOCIAL TASKS

## SOCIAL MEDIA TASK TRACKER

| ACTION/TASK | MON | TUE | WED | THU | FRI | SAT | SUN |
|---|---|---|---|---|---|---|---|
| | | | | | | | |
| | | | | | | | |
| | | | | | | | |
| | | | | | | | |
| | | | | | | | |
| | | | | | | | |
| | | | | | | | |
| | | | | | | | |
| | | | | | | | |
| | | | | | | | |
| | | | | | | | |
| | | | | | | | |
| | | | | | | | |
| ACTION/TASK | MON | TUE | WED | THU | FRI | SAT | SUN |

# CONTENT PLANNER

## BLOG & SOCIAL MEDIA CONTENT PLANNER

| DETAILS | DATE | PLATFORM | DONE |
|---|---|---|---|
| | | | |
| | | | |
| | | | |
| | | | |
| | | | |
| | | | |
| | | | |
| | | | |
| | | | |
| | | | |
| | | | |
| | | | |
| | | | |
| | | | |
| | | | |
| | | | |
| | | | |
| | | | |
| | | | |
| | | | |
| | | | |
| | | | |

# ADVERTISING

## PAID ADVERTISING – PLANNER & TRACKER

AD SUBJECT:   PUBLISHED:   DURATION:

CONTENT:

- [ ] TWITTER
- [ ] INSTAGRAM
- [ ] PINTEREST
- [ ] FACEBOOK
- [ ] OTHER

BUDGET:   CLICKS:   REACH:   VIEWS:   CTR:

---

AD SUBJECT:   PUBLISHED:   DURATION:

CONTENT:

- [ ] TWITTER
- [ ] INSTAGRAM
- [ ] PINTEREST
- [ ] FACEBOOK
- [ ] OTHER

BUDGET:   CLICKS:   REACH:   VIEWS:   CTR:

---

AD SUBJECT:   PUBLISHED:   DURATION:

CONTENT:

- [ ] TWITTER
- [ ] INSTAGRAM
- [ ] PINTEREST
- [ ] FACEBOOK
- [ ] OTHER

BUDGET:   CLICKS:   REACH:   VIEWS:   CTR:

---

AD SUBJECT:   PUBLISHED:   DURATION:

CONTENT:

- [ ] TWITTER
- [ ] INSTAGRAM
- [ ] PINTEREST
- [ ] FACEBOOK
- [ ] OTHER

BUDGET:   CLICKS:   REACH:   VIEWS:   CTR:

# SOCIAL MEDIA

## SOCIAL MEDIA ACCOUNT MANAGEMENT

| SOCIAL MEDIA ACCOUNTS | FACEBOOK GROUPS/OUTREACH |
|---|---|

FACEBOOK.COM/

TWITTER: @

PINTEREST.COM/

INSTAGRAM.COM/

YOUTUBE.COM/

## SOCIAL MEDIA NOTES & IDEAS GOING FORWARD

## OTHER SOCIAL MEDIA ACCOUNTS

| CHANNEL | URL | USERNAME | PASSWORD |
|---|---|---|---|
| | | | |
| | | | |
| | | | |
| | | | |

# SPONSORSHIPS

## PAID SPONSORSHIPS AND REVIEWS

COMPANY / BUSINESS:

PRODUCT

CONTACT

OVERVIEW

KEYWORDS & LINKS

PUBLISH DATE     /     /                         INCOME

NOTES                                            THOUGHTS/OVERVIEW

---

COMPANY / BUSINESS:

PRODUCT

CONTACT

OVERVIEW

KEYWORDS & LINKS

PUBLISH DATE     /     /                         INCOME

NOTES                                            THOUGHTS/OVERVIEW

---

COMPANY / BUSINESS:

PRODUCT

CONTACT

OVERVIEW

KEYWORDS & LINKS

PUBLISH DATE     /     /                         INCOME

NOTES                                            THOUGHTS/OVERVIEW

# CONTENT PLANNER

## SOCIAL MEDIA CONTENT PLANNER

### MONDAY

### TUESDAY

### WEDNESDAY

### THURSDAY

### FRIDAY

### SATURDAY

### SUNDAY

### NOTES & REMINDERS

# POST PLANNER

BLOG POST PLANNER

POST TITLE:

POSTING DATE:

TYPE/FORMAT:   ARTICLE ☐   REVIEW ☐   TUTORIAL ☐   SPONSORED ☐   GUEST POST ☐

BLOG POST OVERVIEW/SUMMARY

| BLOG POST IDEAS FOR THE MONTH | NEWSLETTER/MAILING LIST PROMO |
| --- | --- |

## OTHER PROMOTIONAL CHANNELS

| MONTHLY REFLECTION | IDEAS TO GROW TRAFFIC NEXT MONTH |
| --- | --- |

ADVERTISING & PROMOTION

TAGS & KEYWORDS

RESEARCH

SOURCES

CROSS POSTING & GUEST BLOGGING

SOCIAL MEDIA

FUTURE FOLLOW UP / CROSS MARKETING IDEAS

# NEWSLETTER OUTREACH

## NEWSLETTER TRACKER

NEWSLETTER TOPIC:                                    PUBLISHED:

CONTENT:

# SUBSCRIBERS:                    OPEN RATES:                    CTR:

NEWSLETTER TOPIC:                                    PUBLISHED:

CONTENT:

# SUBSCRIBERS:                    OPEN RATES:                    CTR:

NEWSLETTER TOPIC:                                    PUBLISHED:

CONTENT:

# SUBSCRIBERS:                    OPEN RATES:                    CTR:

NEWSLETTER TOPIC:                                    PUBLISHED:

CONTENT:

# SUBSCRIBERS:                    OPEN RATES:                    CTR:

FUTURE NEWSLETTER SUBJECT LINES & IDEAS

# MARKETING

## ADVERTISING IDEAS TO MAXIMIZE OUTREACH

| SOCIAL MEDIA FOCUS: | MARKETING CHANNELS | ADVERTISING FOCUS |
|---|---|---|
| ☐ INSTAGRAM | | |
| ☐ TWITTER | | |
| ☐ PINTEREST | | |
| ☐ FACEBOOK | | |
| ☐ YOUTUBE | | |
| ☐ TWITCH | | |
| ☐ SNAPCHAT | | |
| ☐ LINKEDIN | | |
| ☐ BLOG | | |
| ☐ | | |
| ☐ | | |

## MARKETING STRATEGY

**CHANNEL**

**TARGET GOAL**

**MARKETING IDEAS**

**ACTION PLAN**

# LINKED IN POSTS

## LINKEDIN POSTS & UPDATE PLANNER

**POST**

| SUMMARY | PUBLISHED    /   / |
|---|---|
| | SPONSORED / PAID BY |
| | REMINDERS & TO DO |
| | ☐ |
| | ☐ |
| TAGS          HASHTAGS | ☐ |
| @          # | ☐ |
| @          # | ☐ |
| @          # | ☐ |

**POST**

| SUMMARY | PUBLISHED    /   / |
|---|---|
| | SPONSORED BY |
| | REMINDERS & TO DO |
| | ☐ |
| | ☐ |
| TAGS          HASHTAGS | ☐ |
| @          # | ☐ |
| @          # | ☐ |
| @          # | ☐ |

**POST**

| SUMMARY | PUBLISHED    /   / |
|---|---|
| | SPONSORED BY |
| | REMINDERS & TO DO |
| | ☐ |
| | ☐ |
| TAGS          HASHTAGS | ☐ |
| @          # | ☐ |
| @          # | ☐ |
| @          # | ☐ |

# INSTAGRAM POSTS

## INSTAGRAM POSTS & UPDATE PLANNER

**POST TITLE:**

| SUMMARY: | | PUBLISHED ON:  /  / |
| --- | --- | --- |
| | | SPONSORED/PAID BY: |
| | | REMINDERS & TO DO |
| | | ☐ |
| TAGS | | ☐ |
| LINKS | HASHTAGS | ☐ |
| @ | # | ☐ |
| @ | # | ☐ |
| @ | # | ☐ |

**POST TITLE:**

| SUMMARY: | | PUBLISHED ON:  /  / |
| --- | --- | --- |
| | | SPONSORED/PAID BY: |
| | | REMINDERS & TO DO |
| | | ☐ |
| TAGS | | ☐ |
| LINKS | HASHTAGS | ☐ |
| @ | # | ☐ |
| @ | # | ☐ |
| @ | # | ☐ |

**POST TITLE:**

| SUMMARY: | | PUBLISHED ON:  /  / |
| --- | --- | --- |
| | | SPONSORED/PAID BY: |
| | | REMINDERS & TO DO |
| | | ☐ |
| TAGS | | ☐ |
| LINKS | HASHTAGS | ☐ |
| @ | # | ☐ |
| @ | # | ☐ |
| @ | # | ☐ |

# PINTEREST PLANNER

## PINTEREST VISION BOARD AND PLANNER

| BOARD #1 | BOARD #2 | BOARD #3 | BOARD #4 | BOARD #5 |
|---|---|---|---|---|
| | | | | |

| BOARD #6 | BOARD #7 | BOARD #8 | BOARD #9 | BOARD #10 |
|---|---|---|---|---|
| | | | | |

**Top Performing Pins**

**What's Currently Trending on Pinterest?**

**Most Popular Boards**

**Pins to Revive**

**Main Keywords**

**Included Elements**

**Notes**

- ☐ BLOG POSTS
- ☐ SPOTLIGHT
- ☐ SPONSORS
- ☐ ETSY
- ☐ TESTIMONIALS
- ☐ REVIEW

# PINTEREST PLANNER

## PINTEREST MARKETING PLANNER

**FOLLOWING**

**DAILY PIN GOAL**

### TOP PINS OF THE WEEK

### TOP KEYWORDS OF THE WEEK

| MONDAY | TUESDAY | WEDNESDAY | THURSDAY |
|--------|---------|-----------|----------|
| KEYWORDS | KEYWORDS | KEYWORDS | KEYWORDS |

| FRIDAY | SATURDAY | SUNDAY | NOTES |
|--------|----------|--------|-------|
| KEYWORDS | KEYWORDS | KEYWORDS | KEYWORDS |

# FACEBOOK PLANNER

## FACEBOOK MARKETING PLANNER

**FOLLOWING**

**TARGET GOAL**

### SCHEDULED POSTS

### TOP POSTS

**MONDAY**

**TUESDAY**

**WEDNESDAY**

**THURSDAY**

TRAFFIC STATS

TRAFFIC STATS

TRAFFIC STATS

TRAFFIC STATS

**FRIDAY**

**SATURDAY**

**SUNDAY**

**NOTES**

TRAFFIC STATS

TRAFFIC STATS

TRAFFIC STATS

TRAFFIC STATS

# YOUTUBE UPDATES

**SUMMARY OF UPDATE**

FILMED ☐ EDITED ☐ THUMBNAIL ☐ DESCRIPTION ☐ PUBLISHED ☐

**SUMMARY OF UPDATE**

FILMED ☐ EDITED ☐ THUMBNAIL ☐ DESCRIPTION ☐ PUBLISHED ☐

**SUMMARY OF UPDATE**

FILMED ☐ EDITED ☐ THUMBNAIL ☐ DESCRIPTION ☐ PUBLISHED ☐

**SUMMARY OF UPDATE**

FILMED ☐ EDITED ☐ THUMBNAIL ☐ DESCRIPTION ☐ PUBLISHED ☐

**SUMMARY OF UPDATE**

FILMED ☐ EDITED ☐ THUMBNAIL ☐ DESCRIPTION ☐ PUBLISHED ☐

**SUMMARY OF UPDATE**

FILMED ☐ EDITED ☐ THUMBNAIL ☐ DESCRIPTION ☐ PUBLISHED ☐

**SUMMARY OF UPDATE**

FILMED ☐ EDITED ☐ THUMBNAIL ☐ DESCRIPTION ☐ PUBLISHED ☐

# SPONSORED POSTS

## PAID SPONSORSHIPS & POSTS

| COMPANY | REVIEW | DEADLINE | EARNINGS | COMPLETED |
|---|---|---|---|---|
| | | | | |

# HASHTAG IDEAS

## HASHTAGS RESEARCH AND IDEAS

**POST THEME:**

Tag #1

Tag #2

Tag #3

Tag #4

Tag #5

Tag #6

Tag #7

Tag #8

**POST THEME:**

Tag #1

Tag #2

Tag #3

Tag #4

Tag #5

Tag #6

Tag #7

Tag #8

**POST THEME:**

Tag #1

Tag #2

Tag #3

Tag #4

Tag #5

Tag #6

Tag #7

Tag #8

**POST THEME:**

Tag #1

Tag #2

Tag #3

Tag #4

Tag #5

Tag #6

Tag #7

Tag #8

**POST THEME:**

Tag #1

Tag #2

Tag #3

Tag #4

Tag #5

Tag #6

Tag #7

Tag #8

**POST THEME:**

Tag #1

Tag #2

Tag #3

Tag #4

Tag #5

Tag #6

Tag #7

Tag #8

# SOCIAL MEDIA

## SOCIAL MEDIA UPDATE TRACKER

**DATE**

CONTENT  PHOTO / VIDEO

OTHER

**DATE**

CONTENT  PHOTO / VIDEO

OTHER

**DATE**

CONTENT  PHOTO / VIDEO

OTHER

**DATE**

CONTENT  PHOTO / VIDEO

OTHER

**DATE**

CONTENT  PHOTO / VIDEO

OTHER

# DATA ANALYSIS

## BUSINESS GROWTH, DATA CHARTS, PROGRESS

CHART FOR:

CHART FOR:

# WEEKLY PLANNER

## MONDAY

☐ BLOG  ☐ TWITTER  ☐ INSTAGRAM  ☐ PINTEREST  ☐ FACEBOOK

## TUESDAY

☐ BLOG  ☐ TWITTER  ☐ INSTAGRAM  ☐ PINTEREST  ☐ FACEBOOK

## WEDNESDAY

☐ BLOG  ☐ TWITTER  ☐ INSTAGRAM  ☐ PINTEREST  ☐ FACEBOOK

## THURSDAY

☐ BLOG  ☐ TWITTER  ☐ INSTAGRAM  ☐ PINTEREST  ☐ FACEBOOK

## FRIDAY

☐ BLOG  ☐ TWITTER  ☐ INSTAGRAM  ☐ PINTEREST  ☐ FACEBOOK

## SATURDAY

☐ BLOG  ☐ TWITTER  ☐ INSTAGRAM  ☐ PINTEREST  ☐ FACEBOOK

## SUNDAY

☐ BLOG  ☐ TWITTER  ☐ INSTAGRAM  ☐ PINTEREST  ☐ FACEBOOK

# WEEKLY PLANNER

**DATE:**

IDEAS, TOPICS, SUMMARY

| BLOG UPDATES/TOPICS | M | T | W | T | F | S | S | IDEAS FOR FUTURE UPDATES |
|---|---|---|---|---|---|---|---|---|
| | | | | | | | | |

# SOCAL MEDIA

## SOCIAL MEDIA SCHEDULE

| | MONDAY | TUESDAY | WEDNESDAY | THURSDAY |
|---|---|---|---|---|
| **FACEBOOK PAGE** | POSTED ☐ | POSTED ☐ | POSTED ☐ | POSTED ☐ |
| **YOUTUBE** | POSTED ☐ | POSTED ☐ | POSTED ☐ | POSTED ☐ |
| **INSTAGRAM** | POSTED ☐ | POSTED ☐ | POSTED ☐ | POSTED ☐ |
| **PINTEREST** | POSTED ☐ | POSTED ☐ | POSTED ☐ | POSTED ☐ |
| **TWITTER** | POSTED ☐ | POSTED ☐ | POSTED ☐ | POSTED ☐ |
| **BLOG** | POSTED ☐ | POSTED ☐ | POSTED ☐ | POSTED ☐ |

# SOCAL MEDIA

## SOCIAL MEDIA SCHEDULE

| | FRIDAY | SATURDAY | SUNDAY | NOTES |
|---|---|---|---|---|
| **FACEBOOK PAGE** | POSTED ☐ | POSTED ☐ | POSTED ☐ | |
| **YOUTUBE** | POSTED ☐ | POSTED ☐ | POSTED ☐ | |
| **INSTAGRAM** | POSTED ☐ | POSTED ☐ | POSTED ☐ | |
| **PINTEREST** | POSTED ☐ | POSTED ☐ | POSTED ☐ | |
| **TWITTER** | POSTED ☐ | POSTED ☐ | POSTED ☐ | |
| **BLOG** | POSTED ☐ | POSTED ☐ | POSTED ☐ | |

# SOCIAL TASKS

## SOCIAL MEDIA TASK TRACKER

| ACTION/TASK | MON | TUE | WED | THU | FRI | SAT | SUN |
|---|---|---|---|---|---|---|---|
| | | | | | | | |
| | | | | | | | |
| | | | | | | | |
| | | | | | | | |
| | | | | | | | |
| | | | | | | | |
| | | | | | | | |
| | | | | | | | |
| | | | | | | | |
| | | | | | | | |
| | | | | | | | |

# CONTENT PLANNER

## BLOG & SOCIAL MEDIA CONTENT PLANNER

| DETAILS | DATE | PLATFORM | DONE |
|---|---|---|---|
|  |  |  |  |
|  |  |  |  |
|  |  |  |  |
|  |  |  |  |
|  |  |  |  |
|  |  |  |  |
|  |  |  |  |
|  |  |  |  |
|  |  |  |  |
|  |  |  |  |
|  |  |  |  |
|  |  |  |  |
|  |  |  |  |
|  |  |  |  |
|  |  |  |  |
|  |  |  |  |
|  |  |  |  |
|  |  |  |  |
|  |  |  |  |
|  |  |  |  |

# ADVERTISING

PAID ADVERTISING – PLANNER & TRACKER

---

AD SUBJECT:     PUBLISHED:     DURATION:

CONTENT:

☐ TWITTER     ☐ INSTAGRAM     ☐ PINTEREST     ☐ FACEBOOK     ☐ OTHER

BUDGET:     CLICKS:     REACH:     VIEWS:     CTR:

---

AD SUBJECT:     PUBLISHED:     DURATION:

CONTENT:

☐ TWITTER     ☐ INSTAGRAM     ☐ PINTEREST     ☐ FACEBOOK     ☐ OTHER

BUDGET:     CLICKS:     REACH:     VIEWS:     CTR:

---

AD SUBJECT:     PUBLISHED:     DURATION:

CONTENT:

☐ TWITTER     ☐ INSTAGRAM     ☐ PINTEREST     ☐ FACEBOOK     ☐ OTHER

BUDGET:     CLICKS:     REACH:     VIEWS:     CTR:

---

AD SUBJECT:     PUBLISHED:     DURATION:

CONTENT:

☐ TWITTER     ☐ INSTAGRAM     ☐ PINTEREST     ☐ FACEBOOK     ☐ OTHER

BUDGET:     CLICKS:     REACH:     VIEWS:     CTR:

# SOCIAL MEDIA

## SOCIAL MEDIA ACCOUNT MANAGEMENT

### SOCIAL MEDIA ACCOUNTS

FACEBOOK.COM/

TWITTER: @

PINTEREST.COM/

INSTAGRAM.COM/

YOUTUBE.COM/

### FACEBOOK GROUPS/OUTREACH

### SOCIAL MEDIA NOTES & IDEAS GOING FORWARD

### OTHER SOCIAL MEDIA ACCOUNTS

| CHANNEL | URL | USERNAME | PASSWORD |
| --- | --- | --- | --- |
|  |  |  |  |
|  |  |  |  |
|  |  |  |  |
|  |  |  |  |
|  |  |  |  |

# SPONSORSHIPS

## PAID SPONSORSHIPS AND REVIEWS

COMPANY / BUSINESS:

PRODUCT

CONTACT

OVERVIEW

KEYWORDS & LINKS

PUBLISH DATE        /        /                                    INCOME

NOTES                                                             THOUGHTS/OVERVIEW

COMPANY / BUSINESS:

PRODUCT

CONTACT

OVERVIEW

KEYWORDS & LINKS

PUBLISH DATE        /        /                                    INCOME

NOTES                                                             THOUGHTS/OVERVIEW

COMPANY / BUSINESS:

PRODUCT

CONTACT

OVERVIEW

KEYWORDS & LINKS

PUBLISH DATE        /        /                                    INCOME

NOTES                                                             THOUGHTS/OVERVIEW

# CONTENT PLANNER

## SOCIAL MEDIA CONTENT PLANNER

### MONDAY

### TUESDAY

### WEDNESDAY

### THURSDAY

### FRIDAY

### SATURDAY

### SUNDAY

### NOTES & REMINDERS

# POST PLANNER

## BLOG POST PLANNER

POST TITLE:                                                    POSTING DATE:

TYPE/FORMAT:   ARTICLE ☐      REVIEW ☐      TUTORIAL ☐      SPONSORED ☐      GUEST POST ☐

BLOG POST OVERVIEW/SUMMARY

## BLOG POST IDEAS FOR THE MONTH

## NEWSLETTER/MAILING LIST PROMO

## OTHER PROMOTIONAL CHANNELS

## MONTHLY REFLECTION

## IDEAS TO GROW TRAFFIC NEXT MONTH

<table>
<tr><td>ADVERTISING & PROMOTION</td><td>TAGS & KEYWORDS</td></tr>
<tr><td>RESEARCH</td><td>SOURCES</td></tr>
<tr><td>CROSS POSTING & GUEST BLOGGING</td><td>SOCIAL MEDIA</td></tr>
<tr><td colspan="2">FUTURE FOLLOW UP / CROSS MARKETING IDEAS</td></tr>
</table>

# NEWSLETTER OUTREACH

## NEWSLETTER TRACKER

NEWSLETTER TOPIC:                                    PUBLISHED:

CONTENT:

# SUBSCRIBERS:                OPEN RATES:                CTR:

NEWSLETTER TOPIC:                                    PUBLISHED:

CONTENT:

# SUBSCRIBERS:                OPEN RATES:                CTR:

NEWSLETTER TOPIC:                                    PUBLISHED:

CONTENT:

# SUBSCRIBERS:                OPEN RATES:                CTR:

NEWSLETTER TOPIC:                                    PUBLISHED:

CONTENT:

# SUBSCRIBERS:                OPEN RATES:                CTR:

### FUTURE NEWSLETTER SUBJECT LINES & IDEAS

# MARKETING

## ADVERTISING IDEAS TO MAXIMIZE OUTREACH

| SOCIAL MEDIA FOCUS: | MARKETING CHANNELS | ADVERTISING FOCUS |
|---|---|---|
| ☐ INSTAGRAM | | |
| ☐ TWITTER | | |
| ☐ PINTEREST | | |
| ☐ FACEBOOK | | |
| ☐ YOUTUBE | | |
| ☐ TWITCH | | |
| ☐ SNAPCHAT | | |
| ☐ LINKEDIN | | |
| ☐ BLOG | | |
| ☐ | | |
| ☐ | | |

## MARKETING STRATEGY

CHANNEL

TARGET GOAL

MARKETING IDEAS

ACTION PLAN

# LINKED IN POSTS

## LINKEDIN POSTS & UPDATE PLANNER

**POST**

| SUMMARY | | PUBLISHED | / / |
| --- | --- | --- | --- |
| | | SPONSORED / PAID BY | |
| | | REMINDERS & TO DO | |
| | | ☐ | |
| | | ☐ | |
| TAGS | HASHTAGS | ☐ | |
| @ | # | ☐ | |
| @ | # | ☐ | |
| @ | # | ☐ | |

**POST**

| SUMMARY | | PUBLISHED | / / |
| --- | --- | --- | --- |
| | | SPONSORED BY | |
| | | REMINDERS & TO DO | |
| | | ☐ | |
| | | ☐ | |
| TAGS | HASHTAGS | ☐ | |
| @ | # | ☐ | |
| @ | # | ☐ | |
| @ | # | ☐ | |

**POST**

| SUMMARY | | PUBLISHED | / / |
| --- | --- | --- | --- |
| | | SPONSORED BY | |
| | | REMINDERS & TO DO | |
| | | ☐ | |
| | | ☐ | |
| TAGS | HASHTAGS | ☐ | |
| @ | # | ☐ | |
| @ | # | ☐ | |
| @ | # | ☐ | |

# INSTAGRAM POSTS

## INSTAGRAM POSTS & UPDATE PLANNER

**POST TITLE:**

SUMMARY:

PUBLISHED ON: / /

SPONSORED/PAID BY:

REMINDERS & TO DO

☐

TAGS ☐

LINKS HASHTAGS ☐

@ # ☐

@ # ☐

@ # ☐

---

**POST TITLE:**

SUMMARY:

PUBLISHED ON: / /

SPONSORED/PAID BY:

REMINDERS & TO DO

☐

TAGS ☐

LINKS HASHTAGS ☐

@ # ☐

@ # ☐

@ # ☐

---

**POST TITLE:**

SUMMARY:

PUBLISHED ON: / /

SPONSORED/PAID BY:

REMINDERS & TO DO

☐

TAGS ☐

LINKS HASHTAGS ☐

@ # ☐

@ # ☐

@ # ☐

# PINTEREST PLANNER

## PINTEREST VISION BOARD AND PLANNER

| BOARD #1 | BOARD #2 | BOARD #3 | BOARD #4 | BOARD #5 |
| --- | --- | --- | --- | --- |

| BOARD #6 | BOARD #7 | BOARD #8 | BOARD #9 | BOARD #10 |
| --- | --- | --- | --- | --- |

### Top Performing Pins

### What's Currently Trending on Pinterest?

### Most Popular Boards

### Pins to Revive

### Main Keywords

### Included Elements

- ☐ BLOG POSTS
- ☐ SPONSORS
- ☐ ETSY
- ☐ TESTIMONIALS
- ☐ REVIEW
- ☐ SPOTLIGHT
- ☐
- ☐
- ☐

### Notes

# PINTEREST PLANNER

## PINTEREST MARKETING PLANNER

**FOLLOWING**

**DAILY PIN GOAL**

### TOP PINS OF THE WEEK

### TOP KEYWORDS OF THE WEEK

| MONDAY | TUESDAY | WEDNESDAY | THURSDAY |
|---|---|---|---|
| KEYWORDS | KEYWORDS | KEYWORDS | KEYWORDS |

| FRIDAY | SATURDAY | SUNDAY | NOTES |
|---|---|---|---|
| KEYWORDS | KEYWORDS | KEYWORDS | KEYWORDS |

# FACEBOOK PLANNER

## FACEBOOK MARKETING PLANNER

**FOLLOWING**

**TARGET GOAL**

**SCHEDULED POSTS**

**TOP POSTS**

| **MONDAY** | **TUESDAY** | **WEDNESDAY** | **THURSDAY** |
|---|---|---|---|
| TRAFFIC STATS | TRAFFIC STATS | TRAFFIC STATS | TRAFFIC STATS |

| **FRIDAY** | **SATURDAY** | **SUNDAY** | **NOTES** |
|---|---|---|---|
| TRAFFIC STATS | TRAFFIC STATS | TRAFFIC STATS | TRAFFIC STATS |

# YOUTUBE UPDATES

SUMMARY OF UPDATE

FILMED   EDITED   THUMBNAIL   DESCRIPTION   PUBLISHED

SUMMARY OF UPDATE

FILMED   EDITED   THUMBNAIL   DESCRIPTION   PUBLISHED

SUMMARY OF UPDATE

FILMED   EDITED   THUMBNAIL   DESCRIPTION   PUBLISHED

SUMMARY OF UPDATE

FILMED   EDITED   THUMBNAIL   DESCRIPTION   PUBLISHED

SUMMARY OF UPDATE

FILMED   EDITED   THUMBNAIL   DESCRIPTION   PUBLISHED

SUMMARY OF UPDATE

FILMED   EDITED   THUMBNAIL   DESCRIPTION   PUBLISHED

SUMMARY OF UPDATE

FILMED   EDITED   THUMBNAIL   DESCRIPTION   PUBLISHED

# SPONSORED POSTS

## PAID SPONSORSHIPS & POSTS

| COMPANY | REVIEW | DEADLINE | EARNINGS | COMPLETED |
|---|---|---|---|---|
| | | | | |
| | | | | |
| | | | | |
| | | | | |
| | | | | |
| | | | | |
| | | | | |
| | | | | |
| | | | | |
| | | | | |
| | | | | |
| | | | | |

# HASHTAG IDEAS

## HASHTAGS RESEARCH AND IDEAS

### POST THEME:

Tag #1

Tag #2

Tag #3

Tag #4

Tag #5

Tag #6

Tag #7

Tag #8

### POST THEME:

Tag #1

Tag #2

Tag #3

Tag #4

Tag #5

Tag #6

Tag #7

Tag #8

### POST THEME:

Tag #1

Tag #2

Tag #3

Tag #4

Tag #5

Tag #6

Tag #7

Tag #8

### POST THEME:

Tag #1

Tag #2

Tag #3

Tag #4

Tag #5

Tag #6

Tag #7

Tag #8

### POST THEME:

Tag #1

Tag #2

Tag #3

Tag #4

Tag #5

Tag #6

Tag #7

Tag #8

### POST THEME:

Tag #1

Tag #2

Tag #3

Tag #4

Tag #5

Tag #6

Tag #7

Tag #8

# SOCIAL MEDIA

## SOCIAL MEDIA UPDATE TRACKER

**DATE** ☐ CONTENT ☐ PHOTO / VIDEO

OTHER

**DATE** ☐ CONTENT ☐ PHOTO / VIDEO

OTHER

**DATE** ☐ CONTENT ☐ PHOTO / VIDEO

OTHER

**DATE** ☐ CONTENT ☐ PHOTO / VIDEO

OTHER

**DATE** ☐ CONTENT ☐ PHOTO / VIDEO

OTHER

# DATA ANALYSIS

## BUSINESS GROWTH, DATA CHARTS, PROGRESS

CHART FOR:

CHART FOR:

# WEEKLY PLANNER

## MONDAY

☐ BLOG ☐ TWITTER ☐ INSTAGRAM ☐ PINTEREST ☐ FACEBOOK

## TUESDAY

☐ BLOG ☐ TWITTER ☐ INSTAGRAM ☐ PINTEREST ☐ FACEBOOK

## WEDNESDAY

☐ BLOG ☐ TWITTER ☐ INSTAGRAM ☐ PINTEREST ☐ FACEBOOK

## THURSDAY

☐ BLOG ☐ TWITTER ☐ INSTAGRAM ☐ PINTEREST ☐ FACEBOOK

## FRIDAY

☐ BLOG ☐ TWITTER ☐ INSTAGRAM ☐ PINTEREST ☐ FACEBOOK

## SATURDAY

☐ BLOG ☐ TWITTER ☐ INSTAGRAM ☐ PINTEREST ☐ FACEBOOK

## SUNDAY

☐ BLOG ☐ TWITTER ☐ INSTAGRAM ☐ PINTEREST ☐ FACEBOOK

# WEEKLY PLANNER

**DATE:**

IDEAS, TOPICS, SUMMARY

BLOG UPDATES/TOPICS     M  T  W  T  F  S  S     IDEAS FOR FUTURE UPDATES

# SOCAL MEDIA

## SOCIAL MEDIA SCHEDULE

|  | MONDAY | TUESDAY | WEDNESDAY | THURSDAY |
|---|---|---|---|---|
| **FACEBOOK PAGE** | POSTED ☐ | POSTED ☐ | POSTED ☐ | POSTED ☐ |
| **YOUTUBE** | POSTED ☐ | POSTED ☐ | POSTED ☐ | POSTED ☐ |
| **INSTAGRAM** | POSTED ☐ | POSTED ☐ | POSTED ☐ | POSTED ☐ |
| **PINTEREST** | POSTED ☐ | POSTED ☐ | POSTED ☐ | POSTED ☐ |
| **TWITTER** | POSTED ☐ | POSTED ☐ | POSTED ☐ | POSTED ☐ |
| **BLOG** | POSTED ☐ | POSTED ☐ | POSTED ☐ | POSTED ☐ |

# SOCAL MEDIA

## SOCIAL MEDIA SCHEDULE

| | FRIDAY | SATURDAY | SUNDAY | NOTES |
|---|---|---|---|---|
| FACEBOOK PAGE | POSTED ☐ | POSTED ☐ | POSTED ☐ | |
| YOUTUBE | POSTED ☐ | POSTED ☐ | POSTED ☐ | |
| INSTAGRAM | POSTED ☐ | POSTED ☐ | POSTED ☐ | |
| PINTEREST | POSTED ☐ | POSTED ☐ | POSTED ☐ | |
| TWITTER | POSTED ☐ | POSTED ☐ | POSTED ☐ | |
| BLOG | POSTED ☐ | POSTED ☐ | POSTED ☐ | |

# SOCIAL TASKS

## SOCIAL MEDIA TASK TRACKER

| ACTION/TASK | MON | TUE | WED | THU | FRI | SAT | SUN |
|---|---|---|---|---|---|---|---|
| | | | | | | | |

# CONTENT PLANNER

## BLOG & SOCIAL MEDIA CONTENT PLANNER

| DETAILS | DATE | PLATFORM | DONE |
|---|---|---|---|
| | | | |
| | | | |
| | | | |
| | | | |
| | | | |
| | | | |
| | | | |
| | | | |
| | | | |
| | | | |
| | | | |
| | | | |
| | | | |
| | | | |
| | | | |
| | | | |
| | | | |
| | | | |
| | | | |
| | | | |
| | | | |
| | | | |

# ADVERTISING



| AD SUBJECT: | PUBLISHED: | DURATION: |
| --- | --- | --- |

CONTENT:

☐ TWITTER  ☐ INSTAGRAM  ☐ PINTEREST  ☐ FACEBOOK  ☐ OTHER

| BUDGET: | CLICKS: | REACH: | VIEWS: | CTR: |
| --- | --- | --- | --- | --- |

| AD SUBJECT: | PUBLISHED: | DURATION: |
| --- | --- | --- |

CONTENT:

☐ TWITTER  ☐ INSTAGRAM  ☐ PINTEREST  ☐ FACEBOOK  ☐ OTHER

| BUDGET: | CLICKS: | REACH: | VIEWS: | CTR: |
| --- | --- | --- | --- | --- |

| AD SUBJECT: | PUBLISHED: | DURATION: |
| --- | --- | --- |

CONTENT:

☐ TWITTER  ☐ INSTAGRAM  ☐ PINTEREST  ☐ FACEBOOK  ☐ OTHER

| BUDGET: | CLICKS: | REACH: | VIEWS: | CTR: |
| --- | --- | --- | --- | --- |

| AD SUBJECT: | PUBLISHED: | DURATION: |
| --- | --- | --- |

CONTENT:

☐ TWITTER  ☐ INSTAGRAM  ☐ PINTEREST  ☐ FACEBOOK  ☐ OTHER

| BUDGET: | CLICKS: | REACH: | VIEWS: | CTR: |
| --- | --- | --- | --- | --- |

# SOCIAL MEDIA

## SOCIAL MEDIA ACCOUNT MANAGEMENT

### SOCIAL MEDIA ACCOUNTS

FACEBOOK.COM/

TWITTER: @

PINTEREST.COM/

INSTAGRAM.COM/

YOUTUBE.COM/

### FACEBOOK GROUPS/OUTREACH

### SOCIAL MEDIA NOTES & IDEAS GOING FORWARD

### OTHER SOCIAL MEDIA ACCOUNTS

| CHANNEL | URL | USERNAME | PASSWORD |
|---|---|---|---|
| | | | |
| | | | |
| | | | |
| | | | |
| | | | |

# SPONSORSHIPS

## PAID SPONSORSHIPS AND REVIEWS

COMPANY / BUSINESS:

PRODUCT

CONTACT

OVERVIEW

KEYWORDS & LINKS

PUBLISH DATE      /      /          INCOME

NOTES                              THOUGHTS/OVERVIEW

---

COMPANY / BUSINESS:

PRODUCT

CONTACT

OVERVIEW

KEYWORDS & LINKS

PUBLISH DATE      /      /          INCOME

NOTES                              THOUGHTS/OVERVIEW

---

COMPANY / BUSINESS:

PRODUCT

CONTACT

OVERVIEW

KEYWORDS & LINKS

PUBLISH DATE      /      /          INCOME

NOTES                              THOUGHTS/OVERVIEW

# CONTENT PLANNER

## SOCIAL MEDIA CONTENT PLANNER

MONDAY

TUESDAY

WEDNESDAY

THURSDAY

FRIDAY

SATURDAY

SUNDAY

NOTES & REMINDERS

# POST PLANNER

BLOG POST PLANNER

POST TITLE:

POSTING DATE:

TYPE/FORMAT:   ARTICLE ☐      REVIEW ☐      TUTORIAL ☐      SPONSORED ☐      GUEST POST ☐

BLOG POST OVERVIEW/SUMMARY

| BLOG POST IDEAS FOR THE MONTH | NEWSLETTER/MAILING LIST PROMO |
| --- | --- |

## OTHER PROMOTIONAL CHANNELS

## MONTHLY REFLECTION

## IDEAS TO GROW TRAFFIC NEXT MONTH

<table>
<tr><td>

ADVERTISING & PROMOTION

</td><td>

TAGS & KEYWORDS

</td></tr>
<tr><td>

RESEARCH

</td><td>

SOURCES

</td></tr>
<tr><td>

CROSS POSTING & GUEST BLOGGING

</td><td>

SOCIAL MEDIA

</td></tr>
</table>

FUTURE FOLLOW UP / CROSS MARKETING IDEAS

# NEWSLETTER OUTREACH

## NEWSLETTER TRACKER

NEWSLETTER TOPIC: | PUBLISHED:

CONTENT:

# SUBSCRIBERS: | OPEN RATES: | CTR:

NEWSLETTER TOPIC: | PUBLISHED:

CONTENT:

# SUBSCRIBERS: | OPEN RATES: | CTR:

NEWSLETTER TOPIC: | PUBLISHED:

CONTENT:

# SUBSCRIBERS: | OPEN RATES: | CTR:

NEWSLETTER TOPIC: | PUBLISHED:

CONTENT:

# SUBSCRIBERS: | OPEN RATES: | CTR:

FUTURE NEWSLETTER SUBJECT LINES & IDEAS

# MARKETING

## ADVERTISING IDEAS TO MAXIMIZE OUTREACH

| SOCIAL MEDIA FOCUS: | MARKETING CHANNELS | ADVERTISING FOCUS |
|---|---|---|
| ☐ INSTAGRAM | | |
| ☐ TWITTER | | |
| ☐ PINTEREST | | |
| ☐ FACEBOOK | | |
| ☐ YOUTUBE | | |
| ☐ TWITCH | | |
| ☐ SNAPCHAT | | |
| ☐ LINKEDIN | | |
| ☐ BLOG | | |
| ☐ | | |
| ☐ | | |

## MARKETING STRATEGY

**CHANNEL**

**TARGET GOAL**

### MARKETING IDEAS

### ACTION PLAN

# LINKED IN POSTS

## LINKEDIN POSTS & UPDATE PLANNER

**POST**

| SUMMARY | | PUBLISHED / / |
| --- | --- | --- |
| | | SPONSORED / PAID BY |
| | | REMINDERS & TO DO |
| | | ☐ |
| | | ☐ |
| TAGS | HASHTAGS | ☐ |
| @ | # | ☐ |
| @ | # | ☐ |
| @ | # | ☐ |

**POST**

| SUMMARY | | PUBLISHED / / |
| --- | --- | --- |
| | | SPONSORED BY |
| | | REMINDERS & TO DO |
| | | ☐ |
| | | ☐ |
| TAGS | HASHTAGS | ☐ |
| @ | # | ☐ |
| @ | # | ☐ |
| @ | # | ☐ |

**POST**

| SUMMARY | | PUBLISHED / / |
| --- | --- | --- |
| | | SPONSORED BY |
| | | REMINDERS & TO DO |
| | | ☐ |
| | | ☐ |
| TAGS | HASHTAGS | ☐ |
| @ | # | ☐ |
| @ | # | ☐ |
| @ | # | ☐ |

# INSTAGRAM POSTS

## INSTAGRAM POSTS & UPDATE PLANNER

**POST TITLE:**

SUMMARY:

PUBLISHED ON: / /

SPONSORED/PAID BY:

REMINDERS & TO DO

TAGS

LINKS HASHTAGS

@ #

@ #

@ #

**POST TITLE:**

SUMMARY:

PUBLISHED ON: / /

SPONSORED/PAID BY:

REMINDERS & TO DO

TAGS

LINKS HASHTAGS

@ #

@ #

@ #

**POST TITLE:**

SUMMARY:

PUBLISHED ON: / /

SPONSORED/PAID BY:

REMINDERS & TO DO

TAGS

LINKS HASHTAGS

@ #

@ #

@ #

# PINTEREST PLANNER

## PINTEREST VISION BOARD AND PLANNER

| BOARD #1 | BOARD #2 | BOARD #3 | BOARD #4 | BOARD #5 |
|---|---|---|---|---|

| BOARD #6 | BOARD #7 | BOARD #8 | BOARD #9 | BOARD #10 |
|---|---|---|---|---|

Top Performing Pins

What's Currently Trending on Pinterest?

Most Popular Boards

Pins to Revive

Main Keywords

Included Elements

Notes

- [ ] BLOG POSTS
- [ ] SPONSORS
- [ ] ETSY
- [ ] TESTIMONIALS
- [ ] REVIEW

- [ ] SPOTLIGHT

# PINTEREST PLANNER

## PINTEREST MARKETING PLANNER

**FOLLOWING**

**DAILY PIN GOAL**

**TOP PINS OF THE WEEK**

**TOP KEYWORDS OF THE WEEK**

| MONDAY | TUESDAY | WEDNESDAY | THURSDAY |
| --- | --- | --- | --- |
| KEYWORDS | KEYWORDS | KEYWORDS | KEYWORDS |

| FRIDAY | SATURDAY | SUNDAY | NOTES |
| --- | --- | --- | --- |
| KEYWORDS | KEYWORDS | KEYWORDS | KEYWORDS |

# FACEBOOK PLANNER

## FACEBOOK MARKETING PLANNER

**FOLLOWING**

**TARGET GOAL**

### SCHEDULED POSTS

### TOP POSTS

**MONDAY**

**TUESDAY**

**WEDNESDAY**

**THURSDAY**

TRAFFIC STATS

TRAFFIC STATS

TRAFFIC STATS

TRAFFIC STATS

**FRIDAY**

**SATURDAY**

**SUNDAY**

**NOTES**

TRAFFIC STATS

TRAFFIC STATS

TRAFFIC STATS

TRAFFIC STATS

# YOUTUBE UPDATES

SUMMARY OF UPDATE

FILMED  EDITED  THUMBNAIL  DESCRIPTION  PUBLISHED

SUMMARY OF UPDATE

FILMED  EDITED  THUMBNAIL  DESCRIPTION  PUBLISHED

SUMMARY OF UPDATE

FILMED  EDITED  THUMBNAIL  DESCRIPTION  PUBLISHED

SUMMARY OF UPDATE

FILMED  EDITED  THUMBNAIL  DESCRIPTION  PUBLISHED

SUMMARY OF UPDATE

FILMED  EDITED  THUMBNAIL  DESCRIPTION  PUBLISHED

SUMMARY OF UPDATE

FILMED  EDITED  THUMBNAIL  DESCRIPTION  PUBLISHED

SUMMARY OF UPDATE

FILMED  EDITED  THUMBNAIL  DESCRIPTION  PUBLISHED

# SPONSORED POSTS

## PAID SPONSORSHIPS & POSTS

| COMPANY | REVIEW | DEADLINE | EARNINGS | COMPLETED |
|---------|--------|----------|----------|-----------|
|  |  |  |  |  |
|  |  |  |  |  |
|  |  |  |  |  |
|  |  |  |  |  |
|  |  |  |  |  |
|  |  |  |  |  |
|  |  |  |  |  |
|  |  |  |  |  |
|  |  |  |  |  |
|  |  |  |  |  |
|  |  |  |  |  |
|  |  |  |  |  |

# HASHTAG IDEAS

## HASHTAGS RESEARCH AND IDEAS

**POST THEME:**

Tag #1

Tag #2

Tag #3

Tag #4

Tag #5

Tag #6

Tag #7

Tag #8

**POST THEME:**

Tag #1

Tag #2

Tag #3

Tag #4

Tag #5

Tag #6

Tag #7

Tag #8

**POST THEME:**

Tag #1

Tag #2

Tag #3

Tag #4

Tag #5

Tag #6

Tag #7

Tag #8

**POST THEME:**

Tag #1

Tag #2

Tag #3

Tag #4

Tag #5

Tag #6

Tag #7

Tag #8

**POST THEME:**

Tag #1

Tag #2

Tag #3

Tag #4

Tag #5

Tag #6

Tag #7

Tag #8

**POST THEME:**

Tag #1

Tag #2

Tag #3

Tag #4

Tag #5

Tag #6

Tag #7

Tag #8

# SOCIAL MEDIA

## SOCIAL MEDIA UPDATE TRACKER

**DATE**  ☐ CONTENT ☐ PHOTO / VIDEO

OTHER

**DATE**  ☐ CONTENT ☐ PHOTO / VIDEO

OTHER

**DATE**  ☐ CONTENT ☐ PHOTO / VIDEO

OTHER

**DATE**  ☐ CONTENT ☐ PHOTO / VIDEO

OTHER

**DATE**  ☐ CONTENT ☐ PHOTO / VIDEO

OTHER

# DATA ANALYSIS

## BUSINESS GROWTH, DATA CHARTS, PROGRESS

CHART FOR:

CHART FOR:

# WEEKLY PLANNER

## MONDAY

BLOG    TWITTER    INSTAGRAM    PINTEREST    FACEBOOK

## TUESDAY

BLOG    TWITTER    INSTAGRAM    PINTEREST    FACEBOOK

## WEDNESDAY

BLOG    TWITTER    INSTAGRAM    PINTEREST    FACEBOOK

## THURSDAY

BLOG    TWITTER    INSTAGRAM    PINTEREST    FACEBOOK

## FRIDAY

BLOG    TWITTER    INSTAGRAM    PINTEREST    FACEBOOK

## SATURDAY

BLOG    TWITTER    INSTAGRAM    PINTEREST    FACEBOOK

## SUNDAY

BLOG    TWITTER    INSTAGRAM    PINTEREST    FACEBOOK

# WEEKLY PLANNER

**DATE:**

IDEAS, TOPICS, SUMMARY

| BLOG UPDATES/TOPICS | M | T | W | T | F | S | S | IDEAS FOR FUTURE UPDATES |
|---|---|---|---|---|---|---|---|---|
| | | | | | | | | |

# SOCAL MEDIA

## SOCIAL MEDIA SCHEDULE

| | MONDAY | TUESDAY | WEDNESDAY | THURSDAY |
|---|---|---|---|---|
| FACEBOOK PAGE | POSTED ☐ | POSTED ☐ | POSTED ☐ | POSTED ☐ |
| YOUTUBE | POSTED ☐ | POSTED ☐ | POSTED ☐ | POSTED ☐ |
| INSTAGRAM | POSTED ☐ | POSTED ☐ | POSTED ☐ | POSTED ☐ |
| PINTEREST | POSTED ☐ | POSTED ☐ | POSTED ☐ | POSTED ☐ |
| TWITTER | POSTED ☐ | POSTED ☐ | POSTED ☐ | POSTED ☐ |
| BLOG | POSTED ☐ | POSTED ☐ | POSTED ☐ | POSTED ☐ |

# SOCAL MEDIA

## SOCIAL MEDIA SCHEDULE

| | FRIDAY | SATURDAY | SUNDAY | NOTES |
|---|---|---|---|---|
| **FACEBOOK PAGE** | POSTED ☐ | POSTED ☐ | POSTED ☐ | |
| **YOUTUBE** | POSTED ☐ | POSTED ☐ | POSTED ☐ | |
| **INSTAGRAM** | POSTED ☐ | POSTED ☐ | POSTED ☐ | |
| **PINTEREST** | POSTED ☐ | POSTED ☐ | POSTED ☐ | |
| **TWITTER** | POSTED ☐ | POSTED ☐ | POSTED ☐ | |
| **BLOG** | POSTED ☐ | POSTED ☐ | POSTED ☐ | |

# SOCIAL TASKS

## SOCIAL MEDIA TASK TRACKER

| ACTION/TASK | MON | TUE | WED | THU | FRI | SAT | SUN |
|---|---|---|---|---|---|---|---|
|  |  |  |  |  |  |  |  |

# CONTENT PLANNER

## BLOG & SOCIAL MEDIA CONTENT PLANNER

| DETAILS | DATE | PLATFORM | DONE |
|---|---|---|---|
|  |  |  |  |
|  |  |  |  |
|  |  |  |  |
|  |  |  |  |
|  |  |  |  |
|  |  |  |  |
|  |  |  |  |
|  |  |  |  |
|  |  |  |  |
|  |  |  |  |
|  |  |  |  |
|  |  |  |  |
|  |  |  |  |
|  |  |  |  |
|  |  |  |  |
|  |  |  |  |
|  |  |  |  |
|  |  |  |  |
|  |  |  |  |
|  |  |  |  |
|  |  |  |  |

# ADVERTISING



AD SUBJECT: | PUBLISHED: | DURATION:

CONTENT:

☐ TWITTER   ☐ INSTAGRAM   ☐ PINTEREST   ☐ FACEBOOK   ☐ OTHER

BUDGET: | CLICKS: | REACH: | VIEWS: | CTR:

---

AD SUBJECT: | PUBLISHED: | DURATION:

CONTENT:

☐ TWITTER   ☐ INSTAGRAM   ☐ PINTEREST   ☐ FACEBOOK   ☐ OTHER

BUDGET: | CLICKS: | REACH: | VIEWS: | CTR:

---

AD SUBJECT: | PUBLISHED: | DURATION:

CONTENT:

☐ TWITTER   ☐ INSTAGRAM   ☐ PINTEREST   ☐ FACEBOOK   ☐ OTHER

BUDGET: | CLICKS: | REACH: | VIEWS: | CTR:

---

AD SUBJECT: | PUBLISHED: | DURATION:

CONTENT:

☐ TWITTER   ☐ INSTAGRAM   ☐ PINTEREST   ☐ FACEBOOK   ☐ OTHER

BUDGET: | CLICKS: | REACH: | VIEWS: | CTR:

# SOCIAL MEDIA

## SOCIAL MEDIA ACCOUNT MANAGEMENT

| SOCIAL MEDIA ACCOUNTS | FACEBOOK GROUPS/OUTREACH |
|---|---|

FACEBOOK.COM/

TWITTER: @

PINTEREST.COM/

INSTAGRAM.COM/

YOUTUBE.COM/

### SOCIAL MEDIA NOTES & IDEAS GOING FORWARD

### OTHER SOCIAL MEDIA ACCOUNTS

| CHANNEL | URL | USERNAME | PASSWORD |
|---|---|---|---|
| | | | |
| | | | |
| | | | |
| | | | |

# SPONSORSHIPS

## PAID SPONSORSHIPS AND REVIEWS

COMPANY / BUSINESS:

PRODUCT

CONTACT

OVERVIEW

KEYWORDS & LINKS

PUBLISH DATE        /        /                    INCOME

NOTES                                            THOUGHTS/OVERVIEW

---

COMPANY / BUSINESS:

PRODUCT

CONTACT

OVERVIEW

KEYWORDS & LINKS

PUBLISH DATE        /        /                    INCOME

NOTES                                            THOUGHTS/OVERVIEW

---

COMPANY / BUSINESS:

PRODUCT

CONTACT

OVERVIEW

KEYWORDS & LINKS

PUBLISH DATE        /        /                    INCOME

NOTES                                            THOUGHTS/OVERVIEW

# CONTENT PLANNER

## SOCIAL MEDIA CONTENT PLANNER

|  |  |
| --- | --- |
| **MONDAY** | **TUESDAY** |

**WEDNESDAY**

f
Twitter
Instagram
Pinterest

**THURSDAY**   **FRIDAY**   **SATURDAY**

**SUNDAY**   **NOTES & REMINDERS**

# POST PLANNER

BLOG POST PLANNER

POST TITLE:

POSTING DATE:

TYPE/FORMAT: ARTICLE ☐ REVIEW ☐ TUTORIAL ☐ SPONSORED ☐ GUEST POST ☐

BLOG POST OVERVIEW/SUMMARY

<table>
<tr><td>BLOG POST IDEAS FOR THE MONTH</td><td>NEWSLETTER/MAILING LIST PROMO</td></tr>
<tr><td></td><td>OTHER PROMOTIONAL CHANNELS</td></tr>
<tr><td>MONTHLY REFLECTION</td><td>IDEAS TO GROW TRAFFIC NEXT MONTH</td></tr>
</table>

| ADVERTISING & PROMOTION | TAGS & KEYWORDS |
|---|---|
| RESEARCH | SOURCES |
| CROSS POSTING & GUEST BLOGGING | SOCIAL MEDIA |

FUTURE FOLLOW UP / CROSS MARKETING IDEAS

# NEWSLETTER OUTREACH

## NEWSLETTER TRACKER

NEWSLETTER TOPIC:                                   PUBLISHED:

CONTENT:

# SUBSCRIBERS:                    OPEN RATES:                    CTR:

NEWSLETTER TOPIC:                                   PUBLISHED:

CONTENT:

# SUBSCRIBERS:                    OPEN RATES:                    CTR:

NEWSLETTER TOPIC:                                   PUBLISHED:

CONTENT:

# SUBSCRIBERS:                    OPEN RATES:                    CTR:

NEWSLETTER TOPIC:                                   PUBLISHED:

CONTENT:

# SUBSCRIBERS:                    OPEN RATES:                    CTR:

### FUTURE NEWSLETTER SUBJECT LINES & IDEAS

# MARKETING

## ADVERTISING IDEAS TO MAXIMIZE OUTREACH

| SOCIAL MEDIA FOCUS: | MARKETING CHANNELS | ADVERTISING FOCUS |
|---|---|---|
| ☐ INSTAGRAM | | |
| ☐ TWITTER | | |
| ☐ PINTEREST | | |
| ☐ FACEBOOK | | |
| ☐ YOUTUBE | | |
| ☐ TWITCH | | |
| ☐ SNAPCHAT | | |
| ☐ LINKEDIN | | |
| ☐ BLOG | | |
| ☐ | | |
| ☐ | | |

## MARKETING STRATEGY

**CHANNEL**

**TARGET GOAL**

### MARKETING IDEAS

### ACTION PLAN

# LINKED IN POSTS

## LINKEDIN POSTS & UPDATE PLANNER

**POST**

| SUMMARY | | PUBLISHED / / |
| --- | --- | --- |
| | | SPONSORED / PAID BY |
| | | REMINDERS & TO DO |
| | | ☐ |
| | | ☐ |
| TAGS | HASHTAGS | ☐ |
| @ | # | ☐ |
| @ | # | ☐ |
| @ | # | ☐ |

**POST**

| SUMMARY | | PUBLISHED / / |
| --- | --- | --- |
| | | SPONSORED BY |
| | | REMINDERS & TO DO |
| | | ☐ |
| | | ☐ |
| TAGS | HASHTAGS | ☐ |
| @ | # | ☐ |
| @ | # | ☐ |
| @ | # | ☐ |

**POST**

| SUMMARY | | PUBLISHED / / |
| --- | --- | --- |
| | | SPONSORED BY |
| | | REMINDERS & TO DO |
| | | ☐ |
| | | ☐ |
| TAGS | HASHTAGS | ☐ |
| @ | # | ☐ |
| @ | # | ☐ |
| @ | # | ☐ |

# INSTAGRAM POSTS

## INSTAGRAM POSTS & UPDATE PLANNER

**POST TITLE:**

SUMMARY:

PUBLISHED ON:  /  /

SPONSORED/PAID BY:

REMINDERS & TO DO

☐

TAGS

☐

LINKS

HASHTAGS

☐

@  #  ☐

@  #  ☐

@  #  ☐

**POST TITLE:**

SUMMARY:

PUBLISHED ON:  /  /

SPONSORED/PAID BY:

REMINDERS & TO DO

☐

TAGS

☐

LINKS

HASHTAGS

☐

@  #  ☐

@  #  ☐

@  #  ☐

**POST TITLE:**

SUMMARY:

PUBLISHED ON:  /  /

SPONSORED/PAID BY:

REMINDERS & TO DO

☐

TAGS

☐

LINKS

HASHTAGS

☐

@  #  ☐

@  #  ☐

@  #  ☐

# PINTEREST PLANNER

## PINTEREST VISION BOARD AND PLANNER

| BOARD #1 | BOARD #2 | BOARD #3 | BOARD #4 | BOARD #5 |
|---|---|---|---|---|

| BOARD #6 | BOARD #7 | BOARD #8 | BOARD #9 | BOARD #10 |
|---|---|---|---|---|

### Top Performing Pins

### What's Currently Trending on Pinterest?

### Most Popular Boards

### Pins to Revive

### Main Keywords

### Included Elements

- ☐ BLOG POSTS
- ☐ SPONSORS
- ☐ ETSY
- ☐ TESTIMONIALS
- ☐ REVIEW
- ☐ SPOTLIGHT
- ☐
- ☐
- ☐
- ☐

### Notes

# PINTEREST PLANNER

## PINTEREST MARKETING PLANNER

**FOLLOWING**

**DAILY PIN GOAL**

### TOP PINS OF THE WEEK

### TOP KEYWORDS OF THE WEEK

**MONDAY**

**TUESDAY**

**WEDNESDAY**

**THURSDAY**

KEYWORDS

KEYWORDS

KEYWORDS

KEYWORDS

**FRIDAY**

**SATURDAY**

**SUNDAY**

**NOTES**

KEYWORDS

KEYWORDS

KEYWORDS

KEYWORDS

# FACEBOOK PLANNER

## FACEBOOK MARKETING PLANNER

**FOLLOWING**

**TARGET GOAL**

**SCHEDULED POSTS**

**TOP POSTS**

| **MONDAY** | **TUESDAY** | **WEDNESDAY** | **THURSDAY** |
|---|---|---|---|
| TRAFFIC STATS | TRAFFIC STATS | TRAFFIC STATS | TRAFFIC STATS |

| **FRIDAY** | **SATURDAY** | **SUNDAY** | **NOTES** |
|---|---|---|---|
| TRAFFIC STATS | TRAFFIC STATS | TRAFFIC STATS | TRAFFIC STATS |

# YOUTUBE UPDATES

SUMMARY OF UPDATE

FILMED    EDITED    THUMBNAIL    DESCRIPTION    PUBLISHED

SUMMARY OF UPDATE

FILMED    EDITED    THUMBNAIL    DESCRIPTION    PUBLISHED

SUMMARY OF UPDATE

FILMED    EDITED    THUMBNAIL    DESCRIPTION    PUBLISHED

SUMMARY OF UPDATE

FILMED    EDITED    THUMBNAIL    DESCRIPTION    PUBLISHED

SUMMARY OF UPDATE

FILMED    EDITED    THUMBNAIL    DESCRIPTION    PUBLISHED

SUMMARY OF UPDATE

FILMED    EDITED    THUMBNAIL    DESCRIPTION    PUBLISHED

SUMMARY OF UPDATE

FILMED    EDITED    THUMBNAIL    DESCRIPTION    PUBLISHED

# SPONSORED POSTS

## PAID SPONSORSHIPS & POSTS

| COMPANY | REVIEW | DEADLINE | EARNINGS | COMPLETED |
|---------|--------|----------|----------|-----------|
|  |  |  |  |  |

# HASHTAG IDEAS

## HASHTAGS RESEARCH AND IDEAS

**POST THEME:**

Tag #1

Tag #2

Tag #3

Tag #4

Tag #5

Tag #6

Tag #7

Tag #8

**POST THEME:**

Tag #1

Tag #2

Tag #3

Tag #4

Tag #5

Tag #6

Tag #7

Tag #8

**POST THEME:**

Tag #1

Tag #2

Tag #3

Tag #4

Tag #5

Tag #6

Tag #7

Tag #8

**POST THEME:**

Tag #1

Tag #2

Tag #3

Tag #4

Tag #5

Tag #6

Tag #7

Tag #8

**POST THEME:**

Tag #1

Tag #2

Tag #3

Tag #4

Tag #5

Tag #6

Tag #7

Tag #8

**POST THEME:**

Tag #1

Tag #2

Tag #3

Tag #4

Tag #5

Tag #6

Tag #7

Tag #8

# SOCIAL MEDIA

## SOCIAL MEDIA UPDATE TRACKER

**DATE**    ☐ CONTENT    ☐ PHOTO / VIDEO

OTHER

**DATE**    ☐ CONTENT    ☐ PHOTO / VIDEO

OTHER

**DATE**    ☐ CONTENT    ☐ PHOTO / VIDEO

OTHER

**DATE**    ☐ CONTENT    ☐ PHOTO / VIDEO

OTHER

**DATE**    ☐ CONTENT    ☐ PHOTO / VIDEO

OTHER

# DATA ANALYSIS

## BUSINESS GROWTH, DATA CHARTS, PROGRESS

CHART FOR:

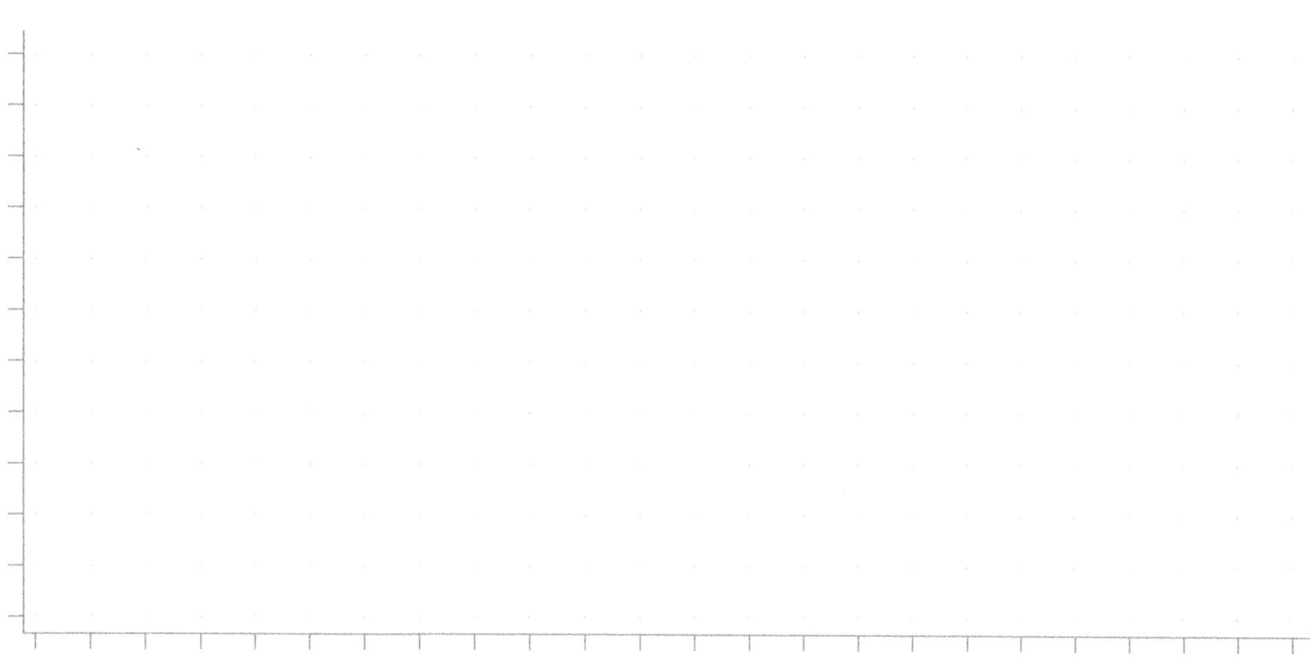

CHART FOR:

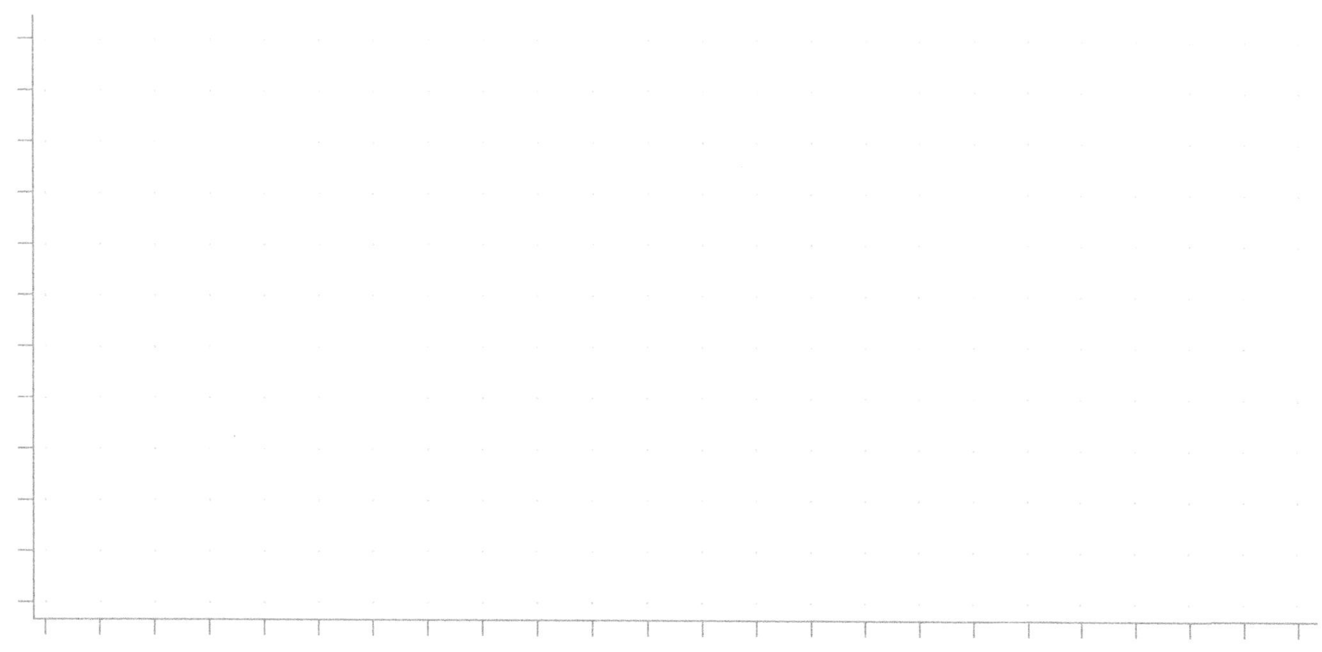

Made in the USA
Monee, IL
07 July 2026

56550991R00090